THE MEDIA MATRIX

Deepening the Context Of Communication Studies

Scott Eastham

UNIVERSITY PRESS OF AMERICA

Lanham • New York • London

University Press of America®, Inc.
4720 Boston Way
Lanham, Maryland 20706

3 Henrietta Street
London WC2E 8LU England

Printed in the United States of America
British Cataloging in Publication Information Available

Library of Congress Cataloging-in-Publication Data

Eastham, Scott, 1949- .
The media matrix : deepening the context of
communication studies / Scott Eastham.
p. cm.
Includes bibliographical references.
1. Mass media. I. Title.
P90.E24 1989 302.23—dc20 89-25096 CIP

ISBN 0-8191-7714-8 (alk. paper)
ISBN 0-8191-7715-6 (pbk. : alk. paper)

The paper used in this publication meets the minimum requirements of American National Standard for Information Sciences—Permanence of Paper for Printed Library Materials, ANSI Z39.48-1984.

for Eric Wesselow

"We make our freedom in the laws we make,
And they contain us as the laws we break
Contained a remnant of an ancient music
That a new music in its laws contains."

Louis Dudek, "New Music" *

ACKNOWLEDGMENTS

Grateful acknowledgment is made to The Macmillan Publishing Co. for permission to cite excerpts from R. Buckminster Fuller and E. J. Applewhite, *Synergetics - Explorations in the Geometry of Thinking* © 1975, 1979; and to Buckminster Fuller's Office in Philadelphia for permission to reprint drawings from the same volume.

I would also like to thank John S. Blackman, co-author with me of *Unfolding Wholes - R. Buckminster Fuller & The Sacred Geometry of Nature* (all rights reserved), for permission to reshape several paragraphs from that book for use in this one. Thomas Parker provided the drawings on pages 112 and 114, and Robert Duchesnay the photograph that appears on page 20.

I am grateful as well to my students and colleagues at Lonergan University College and in the Department of Communication Studies, Concordia University, Montréal, for providing an environment in which the premises of this book could be studied, challenged, corroborated, debated and finally presented here to a wider public.

The Media Matrix

Deepening the Context Of Communication Studies

by Scott Eastham

homo symbolicus
1

tension & compression
13

the symbolic difference
25

the electromagnetic universe
35

resistance, or
'ohms law' of the media
47

the matrix
63

Notes - 79
Appendices - 105
Bibliography - 117

homo symbolicus

Let me stop a moment before I start. What am I going to say? I give myself pause here because, whatever I say, I am about to catch myself on one of the horns of the thorny old dichotomy between theory and praxis. Should I speak only of what is most *important* to us -- the nature of communication and of communications media -- I may fail to communicate what is most *urgent* -- a grave danger threatening human life, human nature and, very possibly, the entirety of Nature. The urgency of the present human predicament takes precedence; all the theories may soon be academic. But maybe there's a connection . . .

We live in what I can only call an epoch of human emergency. The phrase is intended to register on the one hand an *emergency* -- the looming spectre of human extinction through mechanisms of our own devising -- and yet concurrently, the extraordinary possibility of an *emergence*, a new or renewed sense of what it means to be human under these unprecedented conditions.[1] And just what part is played by communications media in the midst of a civilization hellbent on its own destruction? Communication may well be the primary human survival skill, but it is arguable that we are not yet very good at it. We are notably bad, for example, at communicating with people outside our various 'circles' -- our group, our party, our culture, our language, our religion -- or even outside our respective academic disciplines. How are we human beings going to learn to communicate constructively and creatively with one another, for a change, and quickly enough to forestall our own all too readily predictable demise? It's a fair question -- a question of survival.

With outstanding exceptions stemming mainly from the famed Canadian school of communications,[2] the academic study of communication has rather too easily contented itself, it seems to me, with the ready-made utilitarian anthropology of *homo faber*, Man the maker of tools.[3] This instrumental approach goes almost without saying in many areas of study, and contributes to a tendency to consider even the origins of communication from a utilitarian perspective.[4] And it leads to valuable insights; undeniably, we learn how to use certain media more effectively. We become expert at manipulating things -- and people -- to obtain desired 'effects.' From this angle, media of communication are considered to be tools, or else weapons (of propaganda and mass conditioning), simply because the human being is assumed to be primarily an ingenious creature who is continuously inventing new tools and weapons. And indeed, the most direct physical evidence of our earliest ancestors are the stone tools they worked and the bones they left behind. In fact, we have taken it upon ourselves to name this entire vast period 'paleolithic' solely by reference to its primary tool material: the old stone age. But do the old stone tools really tell the whole story?

Not alone, of course not. Yet despite an avalanche of testimony to the contrary from poets, artists, philosophers, theologians and even from pioneering anthropologists,[5] *homo faber* has kept his positivistic perogatives and kept his progressive head above water in the social as well as the 'hard' sciences for most of the 20th century. Alhough many thinkers were discontented with its obvious limitations, no alternative anthropology had garnered sufficient intellectual consensus to unseat old *homo faber*. It was not until Lewis Mumford's ground-breaking studies of the fifties and sixties that other, and perhaps more salient, defining characteristics of the human being began to command a fair hearing amongst students and scholars of technology and culture. It has been an uphill battle; we are a society infatuated by our tools, and entranced by the seemingly unlimited possibilities each new tool promises to open up.

Lewis Mumford, without question the premier historian of technics in North America, had maintained overall a cautious optimism toward most aspects of technological progress until the explosion of the first atomic devices over Hiroshima and Nagasaki at the end of World War II. At this perilous juncture, it became painfully clear to him that if human nature is assumed to be purely the result of our advances in technology, then we have backed ourselves into a deep, dark dead-end: "Gentlemen," he wrote to the U.S. Air Force in 1946, "you are mad."[6] Many of the scientists who worked on the Manhattan Project came to the same conclusion, as you know. Until the H-Bomb, it should be recalled, we human beings have not *ever* invented a weapon we did not eventually get around to using on ourselves.[7] But just how do you go about convincing 'Man the maker of tools' *not* to use one of his own contrivances? It is not in the putative 'nature' of *homo faber* not to use . . . practically anything 'he' can lay his hands on. When Alfred Nobel invented dynamite in 1863, he supposed that with such a terrible weapon in the world's arsenals, nobody could ever countenance waging war again. His contemporary, Dr. Josiah Gatling, is said to have tinkered up the first true machine gun during the American Civil War under the illusion that he was inventing the ultimate 'defensive' weapon. Who would dare attack a position defended by a Gatling gun? In the nuclear age, we are a lot sadder but apparently not much wiser.

Facing humankind's newly discovered ability to engineer its own extinction, Mumford had some very serious second thoughts about those 'stones and bones' and other early implements which were supposed to distinguish human beings from the great apes (who also make and use rudimentary tools in the wild, as it turns out). He came to another conclusion -- or rather, to a different starting point:

> There is good reason to believe that man's technical progress was delayed until, with the advent of *Homo sapiens,* he developed a more elaborate system of expression and communication, and therewith a still more cooperative group life... When we come to the dawn of history we find evidence that makes the pat

identification of man with tools highly questionable, for by then many other parts of human culture were extremely well-developed while his tools were still crude. At the time the Egyptians and the Mesopotamians had invented the symbolic art of writing, they were still using digging tools and stone axes. But before this their languages had become complex, grammatically organized, delicate instruments, capable of articulating and transcribing a constantly enlarging area of human experience.

...Though it was by his symbols, not by his tools, that man's departure from a purely animal state was assured, his most potent form of symbolism, language, left no visible remains until it was fully developed. But when one finds red ochre on the bones of a buried skeleton in a Mousterian cave, both the color and the burial indicate a mind liberated from brute necessity, already advancing toward symbolic representation, conscious of life and death, able to recall the past and address the future, even to conceptualize the redness of blood as a symbol of life: in short, capable of tears and hopes. The burial of the body tells us more about man's nature than would the tool that dug the grave."[8]

So too the oldest human artifact, the eight-spoked 'sun wheel' (so-called) which Louis Leakey unearthed in Olduvai Gorge, shows us that the mandalic 'wheel' pattern was meaningful, and symbolized something important enough to merit carving in stone -- the paths of hunter-gatherers leaving and returning to camp? the organization of families, clans and tribes? the balance and order of the Universe, perhaps? -- nearly 140,000 years before anybody rolled around to 'inventing' the wheel as a practical transportation device.

Mumford was certainly not alone in asserting the centrality of language and symbolic discourse to human life. Linguist Benjamin Lee Whorf defied conventional theory and raised hackles a quarter century before him by declaring that language *constitutes* the human social reality, instead of merely mimicking it.[9] Among Mumford's contemporaries in the sixties, critic Kenneth Burke was expounding an idea of symbolic action in which all participants were co-creators;[10] a notion not unlike the mystical 'participation' of Thomas Aquinas from which Marshall McLuhan drew so many inferences for his electronic 'global village.'[11] In the same era, Bernard Lonergan was reminding the theologians that *meaning* is the fundamental category of all the sciences, natural or human;[12] and philosopher Hans-Georg Gadamer was rediscovering language as the ultimate horizon for a full-fledged hermeneutic ontology: "Being that can be understood is language."[13] In the sciences, meanwhile, as microbiology fathomed ever more profoundly the chemical language of the DNA 'codex,' biologist/anthropologist/cyberneticist Gregory Bateson could refer to the contextual shaping of *all* living organisms as a "grammar," and still be understood by his colleagues: "Anatomy *must* contain an analogue of grammar because all anatomy is a transform of message material, which must be contextually shaped."[14] I am also pleased to note that some Canadian scholars of communication have recently taken up the non-Aristotelian and non-Cartesian social theory developed during this same period by Eugen Rosenstock-Huessy, an outstanding student of Martin Buber's whose approach to the social reality commences directly with the primacy of symbolic relationship and response. "Speech," Rosenstock-Huessy wrote, "sustains the time and space axes of society. Grammar is the method by which we become aware of this social process."[15] It is an axiomatic insight: the symbolic grammar and syntax of communication interweave to form the warp and the weft -- indeed, the entire fabric -- of a culture. If I may borrow one of Barrington Nevitt's lapidary aphorisms, "Culture is communication, and communication is culture."[16]

Otherwise, looking back at the prehistoric

evidence again, how are we supposed to concoct a utilitarian interpretation for the many 'useless' left hands stencilled onto the walls of Magdalenian caves? (See Fig. 1)[17] The utilitarians have already tried to turn the magnificent cave-paintings they accompany into the paleolithic equivalent of game-plans for corporate predators. But such a silhouetted hand, held motionless to the cave wall one day 20,000 years past, stubbornly resists arguments based on utility. This is emphatically not the hand of *homo faber;* it was the other hand, holding a hollow bone blow-sprayer to the lips, that made the painting. The eerie, shadowed hand-print is more like a signature, or a synechdoche: a part standing for the presence of

Figure 1. Stencilled hands from the Castillo cave in the Pyrenees.

the whole person at the sacred site. And when one or more of its fingers have been mutilated by the removal of the top joint, still less is such a deliberately injured hand that of our famous 'handy-man,' *homo faber,* but rather more probably a gesture of grief over the loss of a loved one, or of sacrifice and dedication, common in many primordial cultures even today.

Despite their obvious virtuosity, the artists of the upper paleolithic period made almost no direct *representations* of the human face or figure; the few exceptions to the taboo are masked or deliberately distorted. But with their stencilled hands, the same artists clearly *present* themselves within a context of relationship to the animal powers that made their world meaningful. This is the function of symbols: the presentation of reality, not representations about it -- percepts, not concepts, as Nevitt would have it.[18]

My point here amounts to a miniature thesis in philosophical anthropology: *The human being is that being whose understanding of itself is constitutive of its very being.*[19] Humans are never merely the objects of study, but also and primarily the inquiring subjects. Consequently, no human being and no human culture can ever be wholly objectified. Of course we each understand ourselves in unique ways, according to personal and cultural idiosyncracy. But there is a paradoxical commonality. We come to these understandings always in and through the *symbolic forms* we share with other people: words, manners, works of art, public ceremonies, mass media images, music, dance, architecture, drama, what have you. As Ernst Cassirer more than once observed, you cannot even ask -- let alone say -- what it means to be human without using symbolic forms.[20] Try as you might, you can't jump over your own shadow. Ergo, *homo symbolicus:* symbolic Man: the maker, or more often the finder, of meaning. Cultural anthropologist Clifford Geertz puts it neatly: "The agent of his own realization, [Man] creates out of his general capacity for the construction of symbolic models, the specific capabilities that define him."[21] Which is why whenever human beings set out to define the origin or nature of communication, they find that communication has always already been there, shaping and defining their human nature.

tension & compression

Now what exactly are these symbolic forms? First of all, they are most basically *containers,* not implements. This is an important distinction, although not hard and fast: there is a sliding spectrum of formal values between container and implement. Tools are primarily compressive in structure; containers are generally tensile embracements. Mumford, the great humanist, began his re-assessment of human origins by focusing on the neglected 'physical' containers of human culture -- e.g., the body, the village, the city, the empire -- and, with at least equal emphasis, on the seemingly 'metaphysical' containers: dream, language, ritual, community and, as he saw it, the human mind itself.[22] Containers, he observed, must change more slowly than their contents. They are also intelligible, and may be figuratively 'read' as embodiments of persistent patterns of life, thought, belief or behavior. From another angle altogether, Mumford's scientist/artist contemporary R. Buckminster Fuller was also refocusing current technological practices and priorities by devoting his supremely inventive attention mainly to containers: his one-island-Earth cartographic projection, the Geoscope and World Game inventories of resources, his designs for domed cities and floating cities, the many versions of his geodesic dome-homes, even the self-contained Dymaxion bathroom, all attest this 'encompassing' concern.[23] Fuller and Mumford rarely agreed with one another in later life, but both came to acknowledge words, symbols, images, models, metaphors -- in short, *language* in all its symbolic forms -- as the fundamental container of human culture. Language is the human *mythos* par excellence, the all-embracing horizon within which human life and activities become meaningful and, indeed, human.

As would any good structural engineer, Fuller always took into account *tension and compression* as inseparable and complementary functions of any structural system. When one is at 'high tide' and visible, he would say, the other is always also present, but at 'low tide,' and invisible.[24] Compression is 'push,' and tension 'pull.' If you load a compressive column, its girth expands tensionally at 90° to the direction of the load. If you tense a length of rope, its girth compresses at 90° to the direction of your pull. Tension and compression are always and only co-varying functions. Fuller highlights certain neglected ramifications succinctly in a table I shall include as Appendix I, rather than going on about them at length here.[25] You will notice, however, especially with Fuller reminding you of this 'bias' time and again in his various works, that western civilization has gone about constructing itself almost exclusively by the use of continuous compression -- we pile up bricks to build our houses, we pile up causes to account for effects, and we pile up reasons for our every action. In the things that we build and the ways that we think, the victory always goes to the 'weightiest' argument. Indeed, we use pressure tactics to build everything from architectural structures to logical or legal arguments to political constituencies. As for communication, do we not mostly seek to 'ex-press' ourselves, or to make an 'impression' on others? Can we even imagine any other way to go about it? We tend to trust compressives, which we view as 'hard' and 'solid' realities, while distrusting self-suspended tensional networks -- like the spider's web -- which we view as flimsy and insubstantial. So ingrained is this preference for compressive forces that most of us still feel the wind 'blowing' in our faces when we know very well that it is actually being 'sucked' from behind us. Fuller spent his entire life trying to reverse this structural bias, and designed a collection of truly amazing structures -- I give you the Montréal Expo Dome, his Taj Mahal even today rising above its own ashes -- to demonstrate that 'tensegrity,' or tensional integrity, offers a viable range of alternatives to current 'blockheaded' building practices. And, by the use of continuous tension and discontinuous compression, he did vastly expand our very notions of how to build efficient space-containing systems. Yet he was well aware that he was talking about structures rooted far more deeply . . .

I would suggest to you that this little lesson in structural engineering ought not to be lost on students of communication. Whenever we uncritically assume that communication is a subset of tool-use, we focus our attention and our energies mainly on the compressive dimension of communication. That is, we too often settle for analyzing only forces acting from the outside upon objects, or upon the 'objective' senses of sight, hearing, etc., or upon people reduced to 'objectivity' by demographic surveys or polls. In so doing, we tend to ignore the fabric of connections, the larger tensional embracements which are always also present, and may indeed be the primary structural aspect of communications -- namely, the intrinsic *context:* the community of speakers in a given tradition or mode of discourse, say, or the deeper community of all biological creatures in various interwoven ecological networks or, indeed, the communion of all beings in the mystery of Being itself, if such a language makes sense to you. The visible tool is only a precipitate of 'know-how' *(techné)* and 'know-why' *(psyche)* transmitted down the generations in symbolic forms.

So much of this deep context is still routinely omitted from our academic 'frames' of reference, that it does not surprise me that we remain content to derive the basic thrust of communication studies from the classical models of Greek and Latin rhetoric.[26] All of these are, as Aristotle first noted, basically strategies or analyses or efforts to *persuade,* to bring pressure to bear -- whether logical, or emotional, or physical pressure -- to push people, or political groups, or targeted audiences to respond in certain ways. "If the only tool you have is a hammer," Mark Twain once quipped, "everything begins to look like a nail." The Greeks and Romans built their temples and civic buildings, not to say their respective empires, almost entirely by the use of compressives. Their rhetorical models of communication are constructed in virtually the same fashion:

continuous compression, discontinuous tension: push, push, push. It is perhaps no accident that Albert Speer designed his monumental neo-classical architecture for the Nazi regime along these lines, or that Joseph Goebbels structured his very effective propaganda techniques in much the same way.

Granting the predominance of such models, the entire social fabric is all too often 'imaged' to consist solely of dialectically opposing forces, compressives pushing at each other, while the cohering forces -- the symbolic 'containers' of human culture -- are neglected. Fuller observes that Nature goes about building her structures the other way on, and that she furnishes cyclical and recursive models which are remarkably effective structures even though they seem to defy the familiar one-brick-at-a-time sequences of linear logic.[27] From atoms, molecules and cell membranes to planetary systems and galaxies, Nature uses structures of continuous tension and discontinuous -- Fuller would say 'islanded' -- compression:

> Tension has always been secondary in all man's building and compression has been primary, for he has always thought of compression as solid... Man must now break out of that habit and learn to play at nature's game where tension is primary and where tension explains

> the coherence of the whole. Compression is convenient, very convenient, but always secondary and discontinuous.[28]
>
> Therefore when nature has very large tasks to do, such as cohering the solar system... she has compression operating in little remotely positioned islands, as high energy concentrations, such as the Earth and other planets, ...while cohering the whole system by continuous tension; compression islands in a nonsimultaneous ocean of tension.[29]

The astute reader will already have surmised that tugging or 'pulling' at people's sensibilities must be reckoned very nearly as coercive as 'pushing' or bludgeoning them into submission. The seductive 'come hither' smile, the 'soft-sell' advertisement, the service institution's 'mask of love,' etc., represent merely a tactical shift from overt pressure to slightly more subtle forms of manipulation. Such rhetorical gestures exploit *dis*-continuous tension, and are all the more effective by their apparent contrast to the pervasive media environment of continuous compression. Here, however, we are intending to introduce something altogether different: The *continuous* tension which holds a sonnet or a sonata or a linguistic community together, to take diverse examples, is a comprehensive 'surround' of meaning,

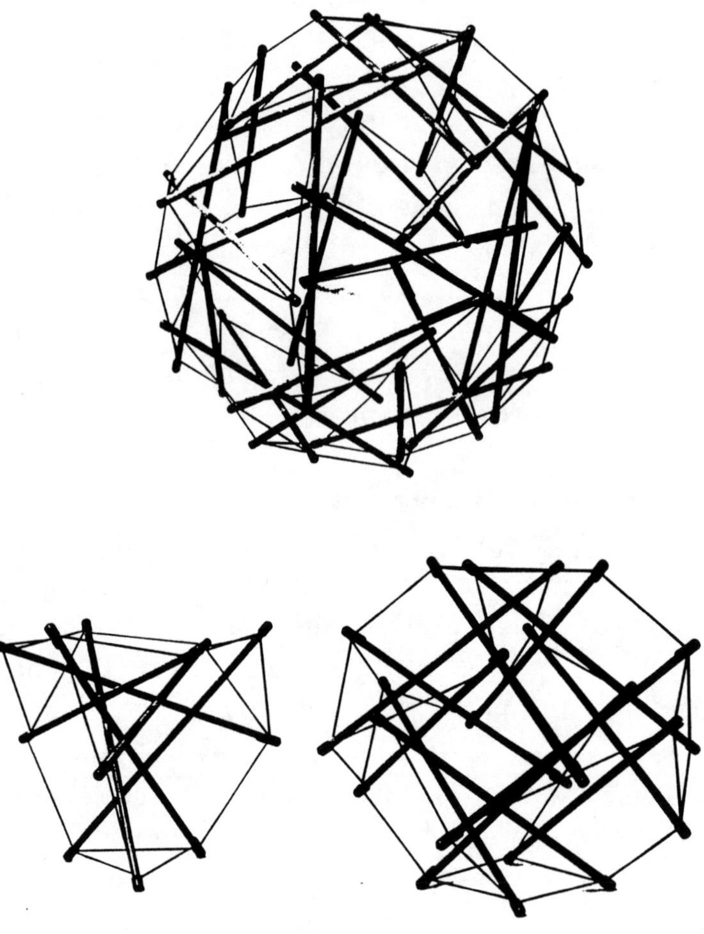

Figure 2. Continuous tension, discontinuous compression.
Tensegrity tetrahedron, octahedron and icosahedron.
Photo by R. Duchesnay; kits by Tensegritoy®

a tensional 'integrity' which should be clearly distinguished from the occasional jerk or yank.

About a decade ago, I wrote a book probing Ezra Pound's unusual 'ideogrammatic' method of writing poems.[30] I discovered that recurrent, non-linear patterns of tensional coherence might very well flay and flaunt the conventions of logical grammar, sequence, narrative, plot, etc., and still make abundant sense. Here is printed literature which flies in the face of the so-called 'alphabet effect.' Even earlier than I, critic Hugh Kenner had also seen the relevance of Fuller's tensional 'great circles' to Pound's work, a phenomenon which he describes elegantly:

> No one can see tension. Newton called one form of it gravity. Another form of it keeps bicycle wheels from collapsing, and another inhabits the clear spaces on a Japanese scroll.[31]

Now given our cultural preoccupation with so-called 'solids,' when we turn to the 'stones and bones' of human prehistory we tend to see only those visible compressives -- the hitting, striking, smashing, cutting, piercing, pounding implements which have resisted the bite of time -- and to ignore the larger, and largely invisible, symbolic networks within which these implements became first of all meaningful, and secondarily, useful. Nonetheless, as noted, tension and compression are always co-varying functions. While we concentrate on the visible compressive elements, we can be sure that the invisible tensional coherence -- the tensile strength in the molecular bonds of a brick or a pillar, for example, or the invisible continuity of a religious tradition's 'pull' upon its adherents -- is equally present, though all too often easy to overlook.

The same critique may be made, unfortunately, of many commonplace assumptions and analyses of communications media and their 'effects.' We tend to think we are dealing with tools that are entirely in our hands, while neglecting their concommitant function as containers of which, again echoing Nevitt and Dennis Murphy here, we ourselves are the content.[32] What Martin Heidegger said of language applies with equal power and pertinence to any symbolic form of human communication we may care to consider:[33]

> Man acts as if he were the shaper and master of language, while it is language which remains mistress of man. When this relation of dominance is inverted, man succumbs to strange contrivances. Language then becomes a means of expression. Where it is expression, language can degenerate to mere impression

(to mere print). Even where the use of language is no more than this, it is good that one should still be careful in one's speech. But this alone can never extricate us from the reversal, from the confusion of the true relation of dominance as between language and man. For in fact it is language that speaks. Man begins speaking and man only speaks to the extent that he responds to, that he corresponds with language, and only insofar as he hears language addressing, concurring with him.[34]

the symbolic difference

"Sprache spricht . . . language speaks," says Heidegger. And what does language speak? It speaks us. Language articulates the constitutive relationships -- biological, personal, familial, community and planetary relationships -- which define us, or more precisely, allow us to get on about the business of defining ourselves. Just so, the image grips the artist, not the other way round; and, at least occasionally in California where I come from, "the music plays the band."[35]

All this sounds passing strange to most western

ears. We are accustomed since Aristotle to defining things according to their differences from one another.[36] We tend to forget, as Gregory Bateson noted, that differences only appear when mapped onto an underlying tautology.[37] Follow me in a short and mercifully simple exercise in symbolic logic. "A does not equal B" ($A \neq B$), the principle of noncontradiction, has been the prevalent pattern of intelligibility in the West for about 2,500 years.[38] We define things in terms of other things: I am not you, left is not right, a chair is not a table, a man is not a woman, etc. But if A did not equal itself first, as it were, and maintain its identity as A, it could not even enter into a non-equation with B. And the same goes for B. Both terms have to be self-identical for their differences (from one another) to be discernable. So much is obvious, no?

But when we come to define symbols and symbolic forms of any sort, neither the logic of difference nor that of identity alone is sufficient to give us the whole symbol. You have to use symbols to talk about symbols. Is there a symbolic definition of symbols? Most attempts confine, rather than define, the symbol. It becomes an arbitrary epistemic sign, a kind of mental arrow, a pointer pointing to something else: "That red light means to stop." The cut-and-dried terminological reductionism of Barthes' semiology, which I investigated at all too tender a young age, left me rather cold; it seemed to be a proliferation of signifiers signifying . . . not very much.[39] I was looking, to paraphrase the title of Dennis Murphy's recent paper, for some school of thought where symbols were taken on their own terms.[40] But no one seemed willing to face the power of symbols without flinching. Moreover, so prevalent is the reigning confusion between signs and symbols in linguistic analysis, that I found myself logging a good number of years in this search for an adequate definition of symbol, one which did not remove my attention from the symbol and direct it to something *else.* Whatever the symbol was supposed to stand for -- a belief, a doctrine, a convention, repressed sexual complexes, latent class struggles, whatever -- such an assertion itself consisted solely of symbols, not of anything else. Hence, more often than not, such definitions merely undercut their own declared significance. Although Cassirer recognized this hermeneutic circle (and potential trap) implicit in any symbolic discourse about symbols, I did not find his neo-Kantian assessment of myths and symbols as "prescientific thinking" particularly just or satisfying.[41] Susanne Langer's "art symbol" gave the symbol a little more autonomy, but equally built in certain 'aesthetic' limitations.[42] For a long while, Jung, Neumann, Hilman and their followers -- most notably Joseph Campbell -- came closest to satisfying me, with their enticing archetypal forms flickering on the "imaginal" threshold between the conscious mind and the collective unconscious.[43] At the same time, as I recall, I was also mesmerized by Norman O. Brown's peremptory epigram: "The symbol is the distance between what you know and what you don't know."[44] So all I knew for sure was that what I was seeking stood at the crossroads between known and unknown, conscious and unconscious, light and the darkness. I just couldn't get across that bridge. When the search seemed fruitless, Paul Ricoeur tried to reassure me that "the symbol gives rise to thought."[45] And so it did . . . interminably.

Then it came to me. I finally learned what every schoolboy knows, or ought to know: "You can't go looking for darkness with a torch." Symbols can poison thinking, too, just as too much or too little thinking can destroy symbols and replace them with concepts or mere 'gut-reactions.'

At that very moment, so to speak, I had the great good fortune to hear Raimundo Panikkar formulating his "symbolic difference." He told me, in brief, that the symbol was simply itself -- precisely the bridge I had been seeking. At last, a symbolic definition of the symbol! I still consider it one of the most important things I have ever heard anyone say. I shall present Panikkar's "symbolic difference" here at some length, and mainly in his own words, because

I have a hunch it may turn out to be a seminal insight for communication studies and related disciplines.

Panikkar intends "to introduce the *symbolic* difference as that existing between the symbol and the reality, i.e., that peculiar difference between the reality (which is, only insofar as it is in its symbol) and its symbol."[46] This is a *sui generis* difference, he says, and not to be reduced to any of the other 'ultimate differences' with which we go about making sense of things. It is not, for example, the aesthetic difference between form and content, itself based on the supposed metaphysical difference between sensuous matter and nonsensuous spirit. It is emphatically not the epistemic difference between knowing subject and known object which renders signs significant: "I know the red light means to stop." Nor is it the epistemological difference between the knower and his or her own knowledge: "I know that I know the red light means to stop." Symbols are not signs. Accordingly, says Panikkar, "The symbol is neither a substitute for the 'thing' nor the 'thing in itself,' but the thing as it appears, as it expresses itself, as it manifests itself."[47] To be sure there is no misunderstanding, he also carefully distinguishes the symbolic difference from the famous ontological difference between Being and beings, as well as from the transcendent or theological difference between

God and beings, and from the anthropological difference between the 'I' and the 'Thou.'[48] The symbol does not mean something *else*, but something *more* . . .

> Symbol here does not mean an epistemic sign, but an *ontomythical* reality that *is* precisely in the symbolizing. A symbol is not a symbol of another ('thing'), but of itself... A symbol is the symbol of that which *is* precisely (symbolized) in the symbol, and which, thus, does not exist without its symbol. A symbol *is* nothing but the symbol of that which appears in and as the symbol. Yet we must beware of identifying the symbol with the symbolized. To overlook the *symbolic difference*, i.e., to mistake the symbol for the symbolized, is precisely *avidyā*, ignorance, confusing the appearance with the reality. But reality is reality precisely because it 'appears' real. ...This real appearance is the symbol.
>
> The symbol is neither a merely objective entity in the world (the thing 'over there'), nor is it a purely subjective entity in the mind (in us 'over here'). There is no symbol that is not in and for a subject, and there is equally no symbol without a specific content claiming objectivity. The symbol encompasses and

> constitutively links the two poles of the real: the object and the subject.[49]

Taking our bearings from this symbolic difference, we see that there are two major directions in which the symbol becomes meaningful to us. Moving toward the 'objective' pole, we are familiar with the symbolic role of the *model* in the sciences, which aims at prediction and transformation of the 'outer' world of empirical causality. Moving toward the 'subjective' pole, we encounter the symbolic reality of the *metaphor,* which aims directly at a transformation of the 'inner' world of consciousness. By the same token, we may also discern that there are always two directions in which to err in the interpretation of symbols: on the one hand *idolatry* (or better, *icon*-olatry), and on the other *iconoclasm*. The first mistakes the symbol for the reality symbolized, forgetting that the symbolized is always *more* than the symbol. The second smashes or throws away the symbol in order to get at the reality symbolized, forgetting that that reality only exists in and through its 'own' proper symbol. Panikkar adds:

> This is why a symbol that requires interpretation is no longer a living symbol. It has become a mere sign. That with the aid of which we would ultimately interpret the alleged 'symbol,' that would be the real symbol.[50]

Now western print culture, it is well known, has long been iconoclastic in the extreme. To the abstraction of the alphabet, it adds the standardized, homogenized repeatability of the printed page, intensifying reliance on a very narrow band of the visual sense alone.[51] The typography of the printed page very nearly forces the reader to pay attention only to the 'content' (the reality symbolized) and to ignore the 'container' (the printed page itself). Marshall McLuhan broke the back of this paradigm with his famous hyperbole that "the medium is the message." Naturally, he was accused of idolatry, or rather of iconolatry: mistaking the form for the content. But you will notice that this criticism places the issue on the footing of the aesthetic (and ultimately metaphysical) difference between a supposedly sensuous form and a supposedly nonsensuous content. If you do it this way, you are forced to take McLuhan literally: You open to the first paragraph of *Understanding Media*. You are told "the medium is the message."[52] You say, "Aha! In that case, the message here is: BOOK." And you close the book . . . on it all. If on the other hand this is a *symbolic* statement (as Nevitt has lately emphasized[53]), the dynamism is maintained between symbol and symbolized. Neither pole is collapsed into the other. The medium is not the (whole) message, but without medium there is no message.

To return to our original problematic, the present epoch of human emergency, we might recall that Jonathan Schell has written: "Extinction is an experience that nobody will ever experience."[54] We have therefore no instinctual, institutional or legal safeguards against this unprecedented danger. Our accelerating technology has opened up new worlds of possibility, as they say, but it has also generated problems in this very world for which there are no purely 'technical' solutions. We now have the technical means to create the conditions of Hell on Earth, to turn this garden planet into a fiery inferno. As Derrick de Kerckhove recently pointed out, the Bomb is utterly *useless* as either a tool or a weapon.[55] Its only function is symbolic -- "the greatest communication medium mankind has ever invented," says he, "not for information but for transformation."[56] We know very well that in order simply to survive, we are going to have to learn to let die away some of the 'identities' -- national, cultural, social, religious and 'individual' identities -- we have so long held so precious that they now imperil the whole Earth. The looming possibility of human extinction poses one fundamental question: What does it means to be human? I submit that in the nuclear age, our identification of human nature with tool-use has outlived its usefulness. For *homo faber*, this is the end of the line; there is no way out. If we use the Bomb, we extinguish ourselves. If we do not end by using the

Bomb, we will have extinguished the dominion of tool-use as the primary defining characteristic of human being. I would contend that unless or until we are able to experience the predictable Megadeath of *homo faber* symbolically, metaphorically, even liturgically -- i.e., in such a way as to find renewal -- then we may very well have doomed our species to pass away physically, literally, and irredeemably. It is this profoundly symbolic character of human experience, catalyzing both memory (the past) and imagination (the future), which may well turn out to be the last best hope for humankind to transform its present perilous predicament.[57]

The urgent has brought us full circle to the important. The *emergency* confronting Man the maker of tools and weapons has led us to detect the *emergence* of symbolic Man as the original face behind the mask of merely technical prowess. Standing at the precipice of species-specific suicide, we find ourselves on the brink of realizing the old Zen koan: "What was your face before you were born?" We see now that our responses to the urgent *(praxis)* will be ineffectual unless we are also able to fully integrate the important *(theoria)*, namely, the nature of communications media.

the electromagnetic universe

In 1912, Ezra Pound wrote: "Energy creates pattern."[58] In an essay called "Medievalism" published in 1931, he was more specific:

> For the modern scientist energy has no borders, it is a shapeless 'mass' of force; even his capacity to differentiate it to a degree never dreamed by the ancients has not led him to think of its shape or even its loci. The rose that his magnet makes in the iron filings, does not lead him to think of the force as floral and extant *(ex stare)*.

> A medieval 'natural philosopher' would find this modern world full of enchantments, not only the light in the electric bulb, but the thought of the current hidden in air and in wire would give him a mind full of forms... The medieval philosopher would probably have been unable to think of the electric world, and *not* think of it as a world of forms. Perhaps algebra has queered our geometry... Or possibly, this will fall under the eye of a contemporary scientist of genius who will answer: But, damn you, that is exactly what we do feel; or under the eye of a painter who will answer: Confound you, you *ought* to find just that in my painting.[59]

Over a period of about 60 years, from the late 1860s to the late 1920s, one might have observed an entire cosmology collapsing, and a new cosmology in the throes of birth. This was emphatically what 'modernism' meant to many of the poets and artists who flew under that banner in the early years of this century. It meant taking leave not only of Victorian fustian and representational imagery, but taking leave also of the static, mechanistic Newtonian universe and immersing oneself in the organic rhythms of the dynamic, wholly energetic Universe heralded by Einstein's famous little equation of $E=mc^2$. So many now familiar theories and discoveries in the sciences combined to form this period, and so many new communications media resulted from them, that I shall provide a table listing some of the main ones as Appendix II rather than enumerating them here.[60]

Particularly for the 'teens and twenties of this 20th Century, it may suffice to say that the atmosphere was 'charged' with the news that the entire Universe of our experience consists of electromagnetic energy, either concentrated as matter or dispersed as radiation. Instead of Newton's Universe, where the norm was a body 'at rest,' the norm in Einstein's Universe is the speed of light expanding in a spherical wave at 186,000 miles per second in every direction. It is a Universe of flux, transformation, metamorphosis. For the astrophysicists, it is an 'isotropic' universe.[61] That is to say, anywhere you may care to position yourself, you will see superclusters and galaxies racing away from you at the speed of light. The Universe has therefore no shape, no 'outside' -- it is not a mechanistic system, but a constantly unfolding scenario. There is in such a relativistic Universe no fixed center or point of view -- or, putting it rather more palatably, the center is everywhere and every viewpoint equally relevant. As for matter, all that 'hard,' durable stuff we took for granted for so long, matter ends up being mainly a matter of perspective. The 'material' world turns out to consist entirely of tightly wound concatenations of electromagnetic energy, still buzzing around in these micro-patterns at 186,000 miles per second. This is a dynamic world of 'events,' not a static world of 'objects.' 'Things' do not just sit there: they happen. It is the most thoroughgoing shift in worldview since the early empirical scientists rejected the medieval theocentric universe and set about designing one of their own, on purely human, rational and quantifiable terms.

Indeed, as Pound correctly intuited, the new universe of electromagnetic energy had much in common with that of the *illuminati,* the light philosophers of the brilliant but abandoned medieval cosmos. Pound himself tried to retrieve Dante's Paradiso as "a single elaborated metaphor on the theme of light,"[62] and liked to cite the 12th Century contemplative, Richard of St. Victor, to the effect that "All things that are, are lights."[63] But there is a marked difference in emphasis. Artists and scientists alike in the 20th Century were not so much looking for a transcendent source of the light, a Father of Lights, as they were seeking to understand and express and even to harness the immanent energy patterns they found in "the things themselves."[64]

All of this had, as we know very well, the most profound consequences in the arts. I may assume that the present audience is familiar with all the ferment and experimentation in the arts during the early part of the 20th Century. At its source, I submit, is a single intuition. I may sum it up in very short order: *All media are electric media.* The electromagnetic universe is itself the primary *container*. . . the matrix of all the media derived from it. I am to this day dismayed anew every time one of my students reveals that he or she supposes the only electric media are the sort that you plug into the wall socket. It means they have missed one of the crucial intuitions from the modernists that sparked McLuhan and his circle to investigate the media of communication in a new way.

Granting that these early communication studies retained a primary emphasis on media as tools, or extensions of Man (as *homo faber),* there also dawned the realization common to the modernists that media were at least equally *environments,* that is, habitable and intelligible subdivisions of Universe. If the former (analytical) approach emphasizes the discontinuity between human products and natural processes, the latter (artistic) approach underscores the continuities between these symbolic microcosms and the surrounding macrocosm.[65] In T. S. Eliot's critical essays like "Tradition and the Individual Talent" (1919), to put but a single example, *tradition* meant precisely such a symbolic container of human experience: a cultural, linguistic and religious environment which each individual contribution alters ever so slightly, and ever so irrevocably.[66]

I should state once and for all that I do not wish to throw out altogether the notion of media as tools, compressive or 'out-pressing' extensions of Man, but only to further explore the intuition that they are also, simultaneously and I would say pre-eminently, tensile containers, 'sub-tendings' of the environing Universe. Tension and compression are always co-varying functions, but to emphasize one or the other makes all the difference. Regarding media as expropriations of the human body leads one to see the entire technological world as a Macanthropos -- a gigantic, autonomous human facsimile. Regarding media as appropriations of Universe leads one to see human artifacts as microcosms, a notion common to many traditional cultures: Our prayer sustains this perishing world; our ritual is the dance of the moon among the stars; our song the seagull's cry over the rhythm of the waves; etc.

Marshall McLuhan and more recently Eric McLuhan rightly hearkened to the acute acoustic sensibility of James Joyce -- nearly blind, as you recall -- who heard tribal drums when he listened to the radio, and who signalled epochal change in *Finnegans Wake* by the famous hundred-letter thunderwords.[67] Joyce also fissioned the etym some years before Fermi fissioned the atom, and had lots of fun with the 'Uniquack' of commercial advertising lingo: "His producers are they not his consumers?"[68] But the newly revealed electromagnetic universe of the early 20th Century had other resonances as well, and jolted other artistic sensibilities to respond in slightly different ways. Pound for one (with whom McLuhan corresponded extensively[69]), and some of his cohorts in the multimedia "Vortex" went back not only to the medieval light philosophers but to the ancient Chinese ideograms, which bring forth patterns and entire Gestalts of meaning foreign to the abstract and compressive logical structures of phonetic literacy. His first guide into these Chinese configurations of meaning was Ernest Fenollosa, a European who went East and remained there, in body and spirit. Pound edited Fenollosa's classic little manifesto, *The Chinese Written Character as a Medium for Poetry,* in which he writes:

> The sentence form was forced upon primitive men by nature itself. It was not we who made it, it was a reflection of the temporal order in causation. All truth has to be expressed in sentences because all truth is a transference of power. The type of sentence in nature is a flash of lightning. It passes between two terms; the cloud, and the earth. No unit of natural process can be less than this. All

natural processes are, in their units, as much as this. Light, heat, gravity, chemical affinity, human will, have this in common: that they redistribute force.[70]

...A true noun, an isolated thing, does not exist in nature. Things are only the terminal points, or rather the meeting points, of actions, cross-sections cut through actions, snapshots. Neither can a pure verb, an abstract motion, be possible in nature. The eye sees noun and verb as one: things in motion, motion in things, and so the Chinese conception tends to represent them. ...The agent and the object are only limiting terms.[71]

...Relations are more real, and more important, than the things they relate. The forces which produce the branch-angles of an oak lay potent in the acorn. Similar lines of resistance, half-curbing the outpressing vitalities, govern the branching of rivers and of nations. Thus a nerve, a wire, a roadway and a clearing house are only varying channels which communication forces for itself. This is more than an analogy. It is identity of structure.[72]

Such an all-pervasive understanding of communication boldly fuses two thrusts of thought in the 20th Century which often seem diametrically opposed. I could call the one scientific or analytic, and the other artistic or humanistic. The emerging cosmology of relativity and quantum physics gives us a Universe in which no phenomenon can be adequately described from a single point of view, or within a single frame of reference. In my book *Nucleus,* I have explored at some length the ramifications of Bohr's principle of complementarity and Heisenberg's principle of indeterminacy, both of which underscore this finite and provisional character of human knowledge.[73] I may therefore be permitted to take a shortcut here by simply pointing out that you cannot properly describe the phenomenon 'butterfly' from either a picture of a caterpillar or a picture of a winged Monarch alone; likewise, the chicken and the egg, the ice and the water and the steam, do not fit into a single frame. Modern physics has discovered no single 'building-block' of nature, and no adequate single 'frame' of reference. As Niels Bohr neatly put the dilemma in 1924: "A complete elucidation of one and the same object may require diverse descriptions which defy a unique point of view."[74]

The artists, on the other hand, knew very well that for human life to be meaningful and integrated, the universe of our experience must be integrated and meaningful. Here is the other dominant thrust of thought in the 20th Century, the integrative tendency. It has perhaps never been expressed more powerfully than by the American poet William Carlos Williams, who wrote in *Spring and All* (1923): "Life is absolutely simple. Everyone should know everything there is to know about life, at once and always. There should never be permitted, confusion --"[75] Soon after this, T. S. Eliot wrote and Pound edited *The Wasteland.* And why is the wasteland the waste land? Precisely because that cohering principle, that integral vision, the very soul of the culture, had bled away, as the life of the Grail kingdom bled away through Amfortas' wound, leaving only shattered monuments, broken bits and pieces, "fragments... shored against... ruins."[76] The following year, Jan C. Smuts published his bestseller, *Holism and Evolution,* which contended that the "real units" of Nature and of culture as well were "wholes" -- the atom, the molecule, the cell, the body, the person, the community, the nation, and so on -- the higher the level of organization and complexity, the greater the autonomy of the "whole" in question.[77]

On the Continent during the twenties, a similar thrust can be felt in the works of philosophers like Martin Heidegger and José Ortega y Gasset who, each in his own way, overthrew the Cartesian subject/object dichotomy and began their thinking from the existential situation of the human being who always already finds himself or herself inserted into a world of meaningful relationships.[78] As Ortega put it, *"Yo soy yo y mi circumstancia,"* I am myself *and* my entire environment.

R. Buckminster Fuller, a scientist-hyphen-artist if ever there was one,[79] first propounded his startling definition of Universe in the same period and in the same spirit -- setting forth not from the viewpoint of the 'self' but from the 'other' pole, the environment:

> Universe is the aggregate of all humanity's consciously apprehended and communicated nonsimultaneous and only partially overlapping experiences.[80]

Such approaches encompass both the subjective and objective poles ("agent and object") by *assuming* the integral and meaningful relationship of human beings to the surrounding Universe, rather than trying (and ever failing) to piece together a synthetic unity by adding up bits of information from specialized disciplines. Thus they assume only that the whole is always more than the sum of its parts, and that the former cannot be derived from the latter. By thinking from the whole to the parts, rather than the other way on, they offer what Bateson called "a pattern of patterns" of articulated relationship: symbolic Man at home in a wholly symbolic Universe.

That situates us. The Universe at large becomes the ultimate context of communication studies, in a sense the 'minimum' communications network, upon which all our own more tangible but more perishable efforts are necessarily overlaid. If it is true that you cannot get 'out' of the Fuller/Einstein Universe, it is equally true that you can always find ways to get 'into' it a little more deeply. Emerson anticipated the situation in his essay "The Poet," in 1850: "Things admit of being used as symbols, because nature is a symbol, in the whole, and in every part."[81]

resistance, or *'ohms law'* of the media

To recapitulate: After $E=mc^2$, the artists become aware that all media are electric media. The energy is tied up into synergetic knots (material) of various frequencies (density).[82] Every medium therefore offers a certain degree of *resistance,* which sounds like but is not quite what Harold Innis meant by the material 'bias' of the medium. Innis saw media somewhat as an economist spies market 'trends,' as indicators for assessing the mainstream socio-cultural effects generated by going along with this bias. He did not look crossways at media, the way the artist looks -- at what you can do in spite of the bias, by stretching the limits, cutting across the grain so to speak, resisting the intrinsic resistances of the medium. In his *Letters,* Marshall McLuhan bluntly noted Innis' shortcomings in this respect: "Harold Innis...had no training whatever in the arts, and this was his gross defect."[83]

The sculptor struggles with the hardness of stone, the musician with the friction of the bow drawn across the strings, the dancer with the limitations of human muscles and sinew, the poet with the lineal sequences of alphabet and typographical page. But all in order that the obdurate marble should appear to flow, the wooden mandicello to sing, the earthbound body to fly and the very soul to find a voice. For the artist, any medium offers its quotient of resistance which, besides being a 'limitation' inherent to the container, also provides the conditions for intensity, measure, and proportion.[84]

Ezra Pound once paraphrased Ohms Law, ordinarily a measure of resistance in an electrical circuit, to underscore this factor of 'resistance' in the communicative arts: *"The electric current gives light where it meets resistance."*[85] The statement makes great sense both literally and metaphorically. The electric current, passing through a resistant medium (e.g., a tungsten filament), heats it to incandescence, producing visible light. But Pound intended it also to apply metaphorically to all artistic media -- considered as sources not of visible light, but of illumination or enlightenment. Observe also the range implied here. Little or no resistance, and the current flows 'normally': no light. But too much resistance will cause a 'short circuit': a brilliant blue-white flash, perhaps, then darkness.

McLuhan also alluded to this 'non-conformism' of the arts and the artist in one of the most durable chapters of *Understanding Media,* "Challenge and Collapse." The artist first confronts the reorientation of the human sensorium precipitated by any new medium, and overcomes the "Narcissus Narcosis" by reappropriating the indigenous resources the new medium has put to sleep -- one's own senses, for example, or one's cultural heritage:

> The new media and technologies by which we amplify and extend ourselves constitute huge collective surgery carried out on the social body with complete disregard for antiseptics. ...For in operating on society with a new technology, it is not the incised area that is most affected. The area of impact and incision is numb. It is the entire system that is changed. ...Each new impact shifts the ratios among all the senses. ...No society has ever known

> enough about its actions to have developed immunity to its new extensions or technologies. Today we have begun to sense that art may be able to provide such immunity.
>
> ...The artist picks up the message of cultural and technological challenge decades before its transforming impact occurs. He...builds models or Noah's arks for facing the change at hand.
>
> ...The percussed victims of the new technology have invariably muttered clichés about the impracticality of artists and their fanciful preferences. But...the ability of the artist to sidestep the bully blow of new technology of any age, and to parry such violence with full awareness, is age-old. ...The artist is the man in any field, scientific or humanistic, who grasps the implications of his actions and of new knowledge in his own time. He is the man of integral awareness.[86]

Is this not precisely how McLuhan saw himself and the role of his work? At any rate, artists are contrary types. Besides picking up on new media, they also pick up discarded or 'obsolesced' media and start to do strange things with them. Notice that when a medium -- speech early on, for example, print for several centuries, and now no doubt television -- becomes a dominant medium, serving as the 'mainline carrier' of a culture's sense of itself, then the medium is indeed the main message, much more important in the subliminal structures it imposes than is the content it purports to carry. At such a moment, its 'bias' is assumed to be universal, and therefore goes almost unnoticed. But when a medium is obsolesced by a new 'mainline carrier,' the artists pick it up and turn it against its general bias, turning it thereby into a vehicle for wide-ranging cultural critiques.

Today, as Brian Fawcett not long ago remarked, writing a book can be a revolutionary act.[87] This subversive potential of the book really first came into its own as films and radio began to replace newspaper and novel-reading in the twenties, which is one reason why the written literature of that period is rife with invention and experiment. Resistance movements, subversive activities . . . A generation earlier, confronting Daguerre's photographs, painters tore up the rule book and began to look at color and design in entirely new ways. Why so much feverish activity in an 'obsolete' medium? Because painting was no longer 'responsible' for propping up the representational worldview and fixed point of view by which western culture had come to recognize itself, and thereafter became critical of the culture at large. And once television appeared to tell the world its tall tales in the fifties, the narrative conventions of cinema were quickly tossed overboard, and New Wave began to happen. Nowadays we're beginning to glimpse the extent to which the computer, and the concommitant digitization of everything and anything, may soon be transforming and perhaps also artistically liberating the so far nearly stillborn medium of television. Such transformations are going on all the time, all around us. Listen to what happens when improvisational keyboard genius Keith Jarrett puts himself under the discipline of playing a full-length concert consisting solely of old jazz *Standards;* new and higher standards of excellence are set.[88] Or look at the oblique light shed when avant garde novelist John Fowles takes on the stodgy form of the Victorian novel in *The French Lieutenant's Woman,* or composes *A Maggot* entirely in early 18th Century English.[89] Examples abound, but for our purposes in communication studies, perhaps one need only consider that Marshall McLuhan wrote *books,* as did nearly all of his most prominent students and colleagues. In fact one of his lesser known books, *From Cliché to Archetype,* specifically details this process: "Obsolescence is not the end of anything... the cultural midden-heap of cast-off clichés and obsolescent forms is the matrix of all innovation."[90]

Perhaps I am only proposing a coda to the McLuhans' now familiar 'tetrad' of media laws, underscoring in particular the subliminal tension between obsolescence, retrieval and reversal.[91] If all media are electric media, our metaphorical 'Ohms Law' applies equally to all of them: the current gives light where it meets resistance, not by conforming to the 'drift.' Consider a film like G. Reggio's *Koyaanasqatsi*, a powerful critique of technological civilization which is itself a highly sophisticated technological artifact. Or consider the enthusiastic response to Bill Moyer's remarkable PBS series of interviews with mythologist Joseph Campbell, flaunting the conventional wisdom of the TV programmers that two 'talking heads' talking sense cannot keep an audience awake. Indeed, behind or beneath these very recent instances, most of what we have come to consider the classics -- or rather, 'anti-classics' -- of the modern period operate in much the same way. When cubist, vorticist and surrealist painters dissected our conventional ways of seeing and presented these autopsies of vision as works of art; when composer John Cage gave a concert at Carnegie Hall and played not a single note; when dramatist Sam Beckett staged a play, *Waiting for Godot,* in which nothing happened -- twice; when novelist James Joyce wrote a circular novel, *Finnegans Wake,* where the last line flowed directly into the first -- here, and in every such case, the art of 'resistance' at once takes the measure of the medium, and vastly extends its range of hitherto unrealized possibilities.

What I'm getting at should by now be obvious. The "lines of resistance, half-curbing the outpressing vitalities" of any medium are precisely the tensional elements that hold that medium together as a symbolic container. When the artist resorts to these "lines of resistance," the tensional substructure of the medium is revealed and becomes a conscious thematic element, instead of merely a subliminal influence. Such 'resistance' activity generates not a new ideology opposed to the status quo, but a poem that is really 'about' the art of poetry, a painting that is 'about' the very elements of painting, a film that is 'about' cinematic conventions and their limitations.[92] Of course any such work will always also have its particular 'content,' but the 'container' will no longer be invisible, the figure will not be abstracted from the ground, nor the text uprooted from its context. And this way lies the true resistance . . . not more propaganda and pressure tactics, but the presentation of a different order of things, indeed, an order based upon a recognition of the 'tensional integrity' that connects symbolic forms and natural forms in an intelligible way. "Art is not an adjunct to existence," wrote Laurence Binyon just before World War I, [or] "a reproduction of the actual... FOR INDEED IT IS NOT ESSENTIAL THAT THE SUBJECT-MATTER SHOULD REPRESENT OR BE LIKE ANYTHING IN NATURE, ONLY IT MUST BE ALIVE WITH A RHYTHMIC VITALITY OF ITS OWN."[93]

Today, just on the verge of its collapse, western civilization is beginning to perceive the bias of its entire 'frame' of reference. For two and a half millennia, the West has given precedence to one symbolic container over all others. I call it 'the box' -- the compartment, the department, the apartment, even the pigeonholes we use to classify and arrange the data of experience. Now boxes can be useful, and I don't mean to trash them all. But it has gotten to the point where western peoples can no longer distinguish between the representations and simulations flickering in their rectilinear frames of reference, and the realities these are supposed to 're-present.'[94] The old Gaussian/Cartesian XYZ coordinate grid is still the locus of scientific method, and of gunsights.[95] Martin Heidegger puts the case most dramatically --

> Let us at long last stop conceiving technology as something purely technical, that is, in terms of man and his machines.
>
> ...Our whole human existence everywhere sees itself challenged -- now playfully and now urgently, now breathlessly and now ponderously -- to devote itself to the planning and calculating of everything. What speaks in this challenge? Does it stem merely from man's spontaneous whim? Or are we here already concerned with beings themselves, in

> such a way that they make a claim on us with respect to their aptness to be planned and calculated?
>
> ...The name for the gathering of this challenge which places man and Being face to face in such a way that they challenge each other by turns is "the framework." [*Gestell* [96]]
>
> That in which and from which man and Being are of concern to each other in the technological world claims us in the manner of the framework. In the mutual confrontation of man and Being we discern the claim that determines the constellation of our age. The framework concerns us everywhere, immediately. The frame, if we may still speak in this manner, is more real than all of atomic energy and the whole world of machinery, more real than the driving power of organization, communications, and automation. Because we no longer encounter what is called the frame within the purview of representation...the frame no longer concerns us as something that is present -- therefore the frame seems at first strange.[97]

But not so very strange to scholars of communication, after all. Technology is the domain of the *means;* Heidegger's "framework" is a way of speaking inclusively about this instrumentalization inherent in the technological world which turns the means, the tool, into an end in itself, and all the things of this world into raw material for production and consumption. It is not just one tool or another that alarms him; it is technology as a systematic strategy of prediction and control which first sets upon, then represents, then objectifies, uses and abuses and finally annihilates everything it touches. It produces an ersatz world of manipulable replicas and simulations, while obscuring or obliterating any reality which cannot be forced into the procrustean bed of the dominant 'World Picture.'[98] Scholars of media and culture have charted the multi-millennial evolution of this representational 'frame' of reference from its Greek origins to its revival in the Renaissance system of perspective, from painting to photography to cinema, from television to the screen of the computer VDT.[99] We know we can do many and marvelous things *within* the frame, but we know also that we are severely biased by it. We tend to look for order only inside these bounds, and to see chaos outside. In point of fact, we know next to nothing about the world outside that frame any longer, except that it no longer seems to 'fit' as neatly as it once did into the box.

This tendency to frame reality, this 'calculating frame of mind,' is so built into our culture that we think nothing of it. Western sports, politics, wars, our systems of jurisprudence, economics and government all have this in common: the 'square' is everywhere: we try to fit practically everything into the neat us/them, right/left, black/white, yes/no, on/off, 0/1 compartments with which we propose to divide and conquer reality. The box offers a great deal of resistance to any reality that cannot be clearly delineated in a sharply defined field -- precisely that bounded by the frame. Consequently, we have put ourselves at odds with one another as long as anyone can remember. We have squared off against the Earth and all her creatures as if they were enemies or competitors. We have done our damnedest to cut ourselves off from the entire reality in our presumption that we are entitled to plan, calculate and exploit it -- and to carry this manipulation beyond all limits.

So at home are we in our box that it is not just a feature of our architecture, for example, or of the way we go about 'packaging' everything from pasta to presidents. It is a dominant chord, what I might call an *architectonic* of our entire civilization. Wherever we westerners leave our mark, it seems to be at right angles to the rest of the Universe. Before the European hordes overran the North American continent, to take a familiar instance, the inhabitants managed to live quite happily in triangulated structures (tipis) or round houses (igloos, etc.). Now, everywhere you turn: boxes piled atop boxes, and all of them numbered, mortgaged, taxed and insured to the hilt against anything the rest of reality might throw our way. We live surrounded by our formal preconceptions; we have conditioned ourselves to see them as normal and natural. We are born into a box (cradle, crib and playpen), we spend every day and every night in a box (home, office, automobile), and we generally insist that our remains be buried in a box.

Were we content simply to analyze the effects this dominant rectilinear model has had upon every kind of activity, from the resolution of conflicts to the compartmentalization of knowledge, we should have to conclude that here is a civilization that has quite literally boxed itself in. Today humankind faces global dilemmas and ecological disruptions which simply do not fit into the structures and the strictures of our conventional frames of reference. Either we succumb to these situations 'unmanageable' from a single, rectilinear point of view, or we learn to jettison our too comfortable models and discover other options. The problems of the modern world have jumped right out of the Pandora's box of western civilization, and can no longer be contained by it. The longer we perpetuate the dominion of the frame and the cubical perspective, the more aggravated become the 180° oppositions it inevitably spawns, and the more likely it is that we shall continue to squander whatever time we have left on this planet fighting one another and our common environment. It is high time for a little 'resistance,' of the sort that sheds light . . .

Indeed, when we look as closely as Buckminster Fuller did at all these 90° perspectives and 180° oppositions, it is a wonder we should ever have trusted them at all. The square frame and the cubical box are not even structures; they have no intrinsic structural integrity whatsoever. Unlike a bag or a cup or a barrel, or eggshells and membranes in Nature, the boxes we construct to live and to work in are in a sense just a jumble of tool-making strategies masquerading as containers. In physically constructing our familiar western habitat of bricks and blocks and boxes, we uncritically apply the tool-making principle of continuous compression to almost everything we build -- despite its aesthetic inelegance and gross structural inefficiency. Post-and-lintel architecture only appears 'solid' because the continuous tension we know as gravity keeps the lintels aligned over the posts; it takes only a small earthquake to demonstrate how unstable such arrangements really are. To get squares and cubes to stand up or stand firm, you have to truss them -- that is to say, triangulate them -- by crossing the square faces with diagonals. The triangles form the 'hidden' tensional continuum. (See Appendix III.) Now then, asked

The Media Matrix

Fuller, what do you suppose would happen if we just dispensed with the $90^\circ/180^\circ$ coordinates of the frame and the box and started off afresh with the elegant 60° coordination of triangles and tetrahedra as our basic structural strategy?[100]

the matrix

What happens -- particularly if you're Bucky Fuller and spend the next half-century working it all out -- is that you discover you have got your hands on the same coordinate system Nature has been working with all along. Once the orthogonal framework has been discarded in favor of 60° coordination, the containers you build hold together quite splendidly. And not only do the triangles always hold firm, but through the omnitriangulated matrix they form, Nature doesn't look so chaotic and irrational anymore. Indeed, it all begins to look positively sublime. "The larger whole," as Gregory Bateson once observed, "is primarily beautiful."[101]

To make a long story short, consider Fig. 3, the isotropic vector matrix of Fuller's *Synergetics*.[102] You begin with triangles, articulate them as tetrahedra, and discover octahedral voids popping out between them to form an "oc-tet truss," the strongest load-bearing structure known to engineering. Continuing the procedure to link up all the vertices discloses an X-ray of Archimedes' cuboctahedron, a figure Fuller first dubbed "The Dymaxion" and later Vector Equilibrium, a pattern in which *the tensile and compressive forces are exactly in balance.* You have now arrived at the simplest form of the isotropic ("same everywhere") vector matrix which Fuller called "Nature's Coordinate System;" perhaps the grandest pattern metaphor proposed by anybody in this century. It is, as Kenner notes in his remarkable book on Fuller, maddeningly difficult to draw one of these matrices on a flat page.[103] They are, however, elegantly simple to model, so I shall have recourse to one of his geodesic models to illustrate a portion of this matrix which so stubbornly -- and significantly -- resists adequate representation on the XYZ axes of the flat paper 'framework.'

I shall also have to make short work of the many scientific corroborations now available for Fuller's intuition that Nature is using this matrix, with its 60° coordination in every direction, for her most basic atomic, molecular, organic and astrophysi-

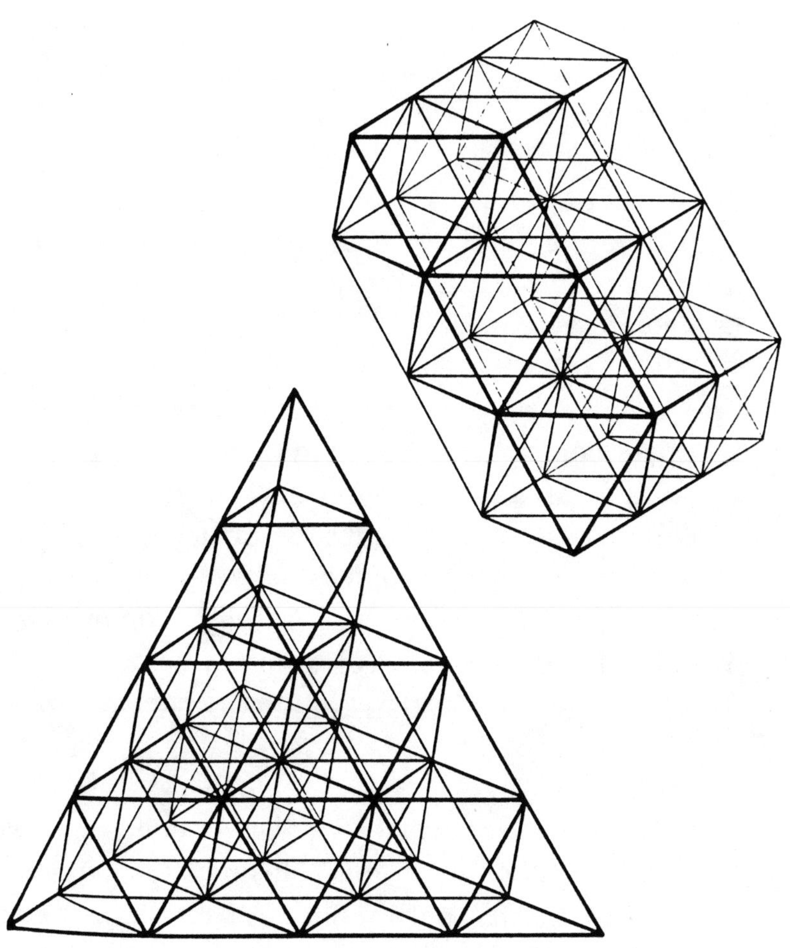

Figure 3. Isotropic Vector Matrices

cal configurations. A few highlights --

- In 1863, Nicholas Van't Hoff discovered that the carbon molecule, and therefore all organic carbon-based chemistry, is tetrahedrally co-ordinate.

- In 1958, Linus Pauling demonstrated by diffraction grating analysis that all metallic (i.e., 'non-organic') structuring is also coordinated tetrahedrally.

- In 1975, Harvard mathematician Arthur Loeb contributed an "Afterpiece" to the first edition of Fuller's *Synergetics* in which he demonstrated that crystal structures of all sorts were accomodated as well by Fuller's isotropic vector matrix as by conventional cubical coordinates. (In point of fact, the cube appears in the matrix, but only as a sort of optical illusion.)

- It is relevant that the DNA code consists always and only of four chemical constituents, and that the helix they generate consists entirely of tetrahedra.

- The geodesic domes which Fuller generated from variations on this matrix turned out to be identical in structure to various viruses and antibody cells.

• The mathematical projections of the strong binding forces of atomic nuclei, which quantum physics terms mesons and baryons, turn out to be vector equilibria and tetrahedra, respectively.

• In 1985 Carbon 60, a remarkably stable cluster of 60 carbon atoms said to be the form of carbon carried by diffuse interstellar gas clouds (and thus the probable seed-form of carbon-based chemistry in the Universe), was synthesized in the lab and named "Buckminsterfullerene" in honor of the man who had predicted its icosahedral configuration.[104]

So there is corroboration aplenty from the sciences that Fuller was indeed on to "Nature's Co-ordinate System" in a profound way. Fuller basically contends that Nature can be so prolifically diverse in reproduction and variation only because she is always most economical in structure. The isotropic vector matrix is derived from the closest-packing of spheres, and therefore models 'least effort' configurations and structural strategies, unlike the cube which distorts and wastes space, time and energy prodigiously. At the center of this matrix is the Vector Equilibrium, the shape Fuller's sees as the true 'zero' of the energetic-synergetic geometry. In order to give some depth to the model provided at the back of this book (See Fig. 4 & Appendix IV), I should allow Fuller to speak for himself about the Vector Equilibrium:

> The vector equilibrium is the anywhere, anywhen, eternally regenerative, event inceptioning and evolutionary accommodation and will never be seen by man in any physical experience. Yet it is the frame of evolvement. It is not in rotation. It is sizeless and timeless. We have its mathematics, which deals discretely with the chordal lengths. The radial vectors and circumferential vectors are the same size.

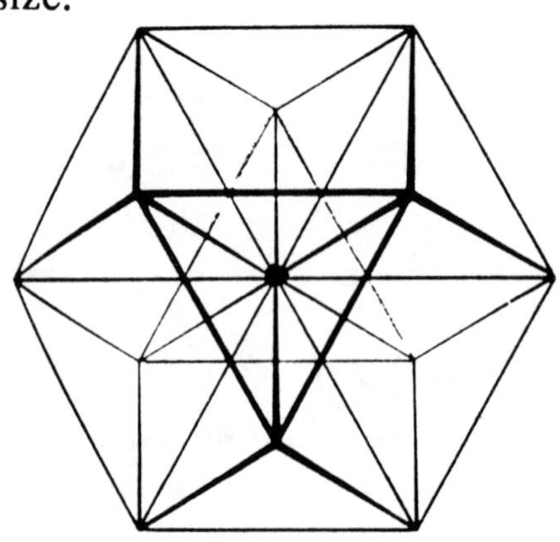

Figure 4. Vector Equilibrium

> The vector equilibrium is a condition at which nature never allows herself to tarry. The vector equilibrium itself is never found exactly symmetrically in nature's crystallography. Ever pulsive and impulsive, nature never pauses her cycling at equilibrium: she refuses to get caught irrecoverably at the zero phase of energy. She always closes her transformative cycles at the maximum positive or negative asymmetry stages. See the delicate crystal asymmetry in nature. We have vector equilibriums mildly distorted to asymmetry limits as nature pulsates positively and negatively in respect to equilibrium. Everything that we know as reality has to be either a positive or a negative aspect of the omnipulsative physical Universe.
>
> ...As the circumferentially united and finite great-circle chord vectors of the vector equilibrium cohere the radial vectors, so also does the metaphysical cohere the physical.[105]

It should be obvious that human building methods would benefit from using Nature's most efficient structures, but that's not the only point. I would submit that human relationships, and therefore human communications, might be more harmoniously articulated if approached according to these omnitriangulated patterns. Instead of conceiving all these relationships in dialectical either/or terms, it is possible to recognize and work within the dynamic of tensions. Barry Nevitt has aptly noted that this amounts simply to human maturity, and contrasted the wisdom of paradox to the one-sided arguments of 'logical' maturity.[106] Instead of looking only for rational or causal 'foundations' on which to build compressive structures, we might also begin to look for 'horizons' of intelligibility which embrace a variety of viewpoints without sacrificing coherence. The media 'containers' we have been discussing are not impenetrable barriers; they are porous, semi-permeable membranes in constant intercourse with other -- internal as well as external -- symbolic environments. Instead of refining only the tools and tactics of classical rhetoric or modern propaganda and advertising techniques, we might once again turn fruitfully to these primordial containers of human culture -- the languages, the works of art, the shared social and religious rituals, the images, models, and metaphors -- by we which understand ourselves as human beings, even today and in spite of all.

"The Vector Equilibrium contains the whole phenomenology of the Universe,"[107] says Fuller, who knew well that this Universe contains structures of very nearly infinite variety. It is the cube and frame which claim to be the single, universal language of science and technology, and which have trapped us in a world which refuses to conform to our calculations. Once we begin to look for alternative patterns, we may also see that such patterns have been celebrated and cerebrated from time immemorial in virtually all the cultures of the world. Every culture has its sacred geometry, its mandalas and yantras (See Fig. 5), its sacred proportions -- not only for the building of temples and cathedrals, but for the orderly integration of the many dispersive vectors of human energy in a given society. Octahedral persian carpets,

Figure 5. Sri Yantra

icosahedral cathedral architecture, tetrahedral hindu meditation diagrams, etc., resemble Fuller's geometry rather than Descartes' because they too draw up their patterns from Nature, rather than imposing upon recursive natural rhythms and cycles the rectilinear, monofocal 'perspective' of the West.[108] Of course nowadays we promulgate our technological framework to every culture in the world under the euphemism of 'development,' so that very soon everybody will see things our way. Or will they?[109]

Now despite his friendly association with Marshall McLuhan, Buckminster Fuller is not ordinarily considered a scholar of communications. When he asserts, for instance, that "triangle is structure and structure is triangle,"[110] and proposes a triangulated geometrical matrix as "Nature's Coordinate System," what possible relevance has such a seemingly abstract model to the issues one confronts day by day in communication studies? A great deal, I would suggest. It impels at the very least a thoroughgoing re-examination of the epistemological models we employ to organize information intelligibly. Here I can only schematize such a project, which reverberates in many fields of inquiry.[111]

We are accustomed to organizing information according either to a monistic or a dualistic epistemological framework. That is, we begin on the one hand by assuming a single (90°) perspective -- that of truth, or of the good, for example, or of scientific experiment and empiricism -- and attempt from this 'overview' to subsume all the data of our experience under that one heading. Or, on the other hand, we assume there are a plurality of viewpoints -- scientific, humanistic, political, religious, economic, etc. -- which vie with one another (in dialectical 180° oppositions) to classify and arrange the data according to their respective priorities. In the first instance, we assert that the one idea, the pattern, order, procedure, or whatever, is so powerful that it will in the end bring all the information into line. In the second model, we assert that the alternative ideas, the variations, even the randomness we find in the data is so overwhelming that no single principle can be found to make sense of it all. In short, we take our epistemological stand on either the one fixed pattern or the innumerable variations. Now, while respecting both the (monistic) perogatives of power and the (dualistic) strategies of dialectics, is it not also plausible to suggest that there might be a middle way?[112]

You do not make music from either a single theme or infinite variations. The music is in the rhythmic interplay between pattern and variation, order and randomness. And it is the same with biological organisms -- in morphogenesis, the genetic pattern is largely fixed but, once born, the growing organism is in the main flexible and open to learning new environmental adaptations.[113] As Arthur Koestler liked to observe, all things subsist in the tension between fixed codes and flexible strategies.[114] Consider the trillions of snowflakes crystallizing overhead and underfoot every winter: they are all hexagonal, and each unique. Here you are glimpsing the matrix of "Nature's Coordinate System" at work -- or let us rather say at play -- "in the whole, and in every part."

I earlier underscored in this regard the importance and centrality of Panikkar's symbolic difference, which understands symbol and symbolized as 'neither one nor two' -- it is the 'same difference,' so to speak. Similarly, I would insist here, Fuller's triangulated matrix implies an entire nondual epistemology of communications based neither on the monistic principle of identity (A=A), nor on the dualistic principle of non-contradiction (A≠B). I shall append a table outlining some of the ramifications of such a nondual epistemology for communication studies (Appendix V). What does it tell us? That we may organize our information according to one single viewpoint, or according to many competing viewpoints, but that neither model will ever be adequate to fully 'contain' the information so organized. Indeed, they are both versions of the cubical 'framework' autopsied earlier. Neither its 90°

perspective nor its 180° either/or polarities can exhaustively model the realities they claim to 're-present.' However airtight our epistemological strategies, they are never ontologically complete. Any reality we may care to communicate or communicate with -- an atom, a cell, another human being, a political community -- is neither one monolithic unity nor many individual entities. The reality here is always symbolic, that is, *more* than the sum of our representations of it . . . It is all relative, and constitutively so. This is not relativism, but relativity: Everything is intrinsically *related* to everything else, and triangulated patterns therefore model the bare bones of these energetic and intelligible interrelationships more adequately than do our customary cubes and frames.

When we turn to these alternative patterns, we begin to see that they sketch the interconnectedness of all life, indeed, "the pattern of patterns that connect" of which Bateson wrote so eloquently, the first and final context. There is an old name for this "pattern of patterns" in the West, nowadays nearly forgotten. It is the *anima mundi,* the so-called 'World Soul,' which we lately see being revived not only in physics and biology, but in the Gaia movement and the various Goddess spiritualities arising spontaneously in our day.[115] Leaving aside for the moment its geometrical elaborations by classical, medieval and renaissance thinkers, or even early scientists like Kepler, it is the intuition that the Universe is alive, animate, 'en-souled.' I have written elsewhere on this topic, and should by rights refer you to that work for further elucidations.[116] I may, however, add this: The isotropic vector matrix presents a new generation or, more properly, *a regeneration of symbolic forms.* It is not a new tool-kit, but the original container: the womb and mother *(matrix/ mater)* of all media. It is not the cause of 'effects,' but the acausal continuum, the 'tissue' of connections. It is not a 'universal' language, but the patterned 'language' of this Universe.

"In nature are signatures," wrote Ezra Pound.[117] As we slowly relearn to read these symbolic forms, in culture as in Nature, we find out what the poets have been telling us all along: Communication constitutes no less than the very structure of this Universe. "Everything is only a metaphor," as Norman O. Brown once put it: "There is only poetry."[118]

###

The Media Matrix

NOTES

* (Epigraph) Louis Dudek, "New Music," *Collected Poetry*, Montréal (Delta Canada) 1971, p. 59.

1. Cf. Scott Eastham, *Nucleus - Reconnecting Science & Religion in the Nuclear Age*, Santa Fe (Bear & Company) 1987, where I have documented this crisis in greater detail than is feasible here.

2. I am thinking primarily of the 'school' (or spectrum) of thought represented by Innis, McLuhan, Carpenter, Hall, Ong, Grant, Nevitt, E. McLuhan, Theall, de Kerckhove, Murphy, et al.

3. I should explicitly state here that when I occasionally use Man with a capital "M," it is intended to refer to "the human being," as do *anthropos, homo, Mensch, homme*, etc., including the aspect of sexuality but not restricted to it or by it.

4. Cf., e.g., Gordon W. Hewes, "An Explicit Formulation of the Relationship Between Tool-Using, Tool-Making, and the Emergence of Language," in *Visible Language*, Vol. VII, No. 2, Spring, 1973, pp. 101-117, which marshalls numerous unverifiable extensions of scientific method into a fairly massive body of self-serving 'evidence' for a utilitarian philosophical anthropology. His argument in abstract:

> "Manual-gestural language evolves with tool-use, and...the vocal-auditory development of speech was a much later, and somewhat secondary effect of the general cognitive enhancement. ...The motor and

> neural elements involved in manipulation of objects and in gestural communication are very similar. The fundamental visual bias of human cognition is stressed."

Hewes himself notes the contradiction: If you are busy gesturing, you are not making tools; if you are making tools, your 'communicative' gestures are reduced to a minimum, except as examples of tool-making. But this does not deter him; he even ventures to predict the future:

> "The connection of tools to language [here he consistently means merely "propositional language"] has taken a most unexpected turn; many of the purposes for which language came into being can now, in principle, be taken over by tools..."

Such a completely utilitarian view perceives nothing but instrumental purposes for language. The "manipulation of objects" supplants the play of the Spirit and the Word and dooms us to be merely the products of our own productions. Hewes therefore deems upper paleolithic art (see below, and Fig. 1) "frozen gesture," and sees it only as a sophisticated notational system, partly for calendrical purposes.

5. Cf. the work of the 'father' of modern anthropology, Edward B. Tylor, on gestural and pictorial language in, e.g., *Researches into the Early History of Mankind and the Development of Civilization,* London, 1865, Chicago, 1964; or Gladys Reichard's classic study, *Navaho Religion - A Study of Symbolism,* Princeton, NJ (Bollingen) 1959, 1963.

6. Cf. Lewis Mumford, "ABC of Demoralization," *My Works and Days,* New York (Harcourt, Brace, Jovanovich) 1979, pp. 436-461.

7. The reader is of course aware of the neutron bomb and various biological weapons which also fall into this dubious category of ultimate weapons 'not yet used.'

8. Lewis Mumford, *The Myth of the Machine,* Vol. 1, *Technics and Human Development,* New York (Harcourt, Brace, Jovanovich) 1967, pp. 22-24.

9. Cf. Benjamin Lee Whorf, *Language, Thought & Reality,* J. B. Carroll, Ed., Cambridge, MA (The M.I.T. Press) 1956, e.g., contrasting English and Hopi:

> "The metaphysics underlying our own language, thinking, and modern culture...imposes upon the universe two grand COSMIC FORMS, space and time; static three-dimensional space, and kinetic one-dimensional uniformly and perpetually flowing time --" (p. 59) ...
>
> "After long and careful study and analysis, the Hopi language is seen to contain no words, grammatical forms, constructions or expressions that refer directly to what we call 'time,' or to past, present, or future, or to enduring or lasting, or to motion as kinematic rather than dynamic." (p. 57)

10. Kenneth Burke, *Language as Symbolic Action,* Berkeley, CA (University of California Press) 1968.

11. Cf. Donald F. Theall, "Messages in McLuhan's Letters: The Communicator as Correspondent," *Canadian Journal of Communication,* Vol. 13, Nos. 3 & 4, 1987, pp. 86-98.

12. Bernard Lonergan, *Method in Theology,* New York (Herder & Herder) 1972, Chapter 3, "Meaning," pp. 57-145, in which he unfortunately also propounds his reductionistic definition of symbols as real or imaginary objects which evoke affects.

13. Hans-Georg Gadamer, *Truth and Method,* New York (Seabury) 1972, p. 432.

14. Gregory Bateson, *Mind and Nature - A Necessary Unity,* New York (Dutton) 1979, p. 17.

15. Eugen Rosenstock-Huessy, *Speech and Reality,* Norwich, VT (Argo Books) 1970, p. 16. "We" become aware of ourselves and our world only in response to one another; the "I" arises in response to the "Thou," and thus "We" sally forth to face the impersonal world of "It" and "Them." Cf. also some of his other seminal works, e.g., *I Am an Impure Thinker,* Norwich, VT (Argo Books) 1970; *The Multiformity of Man,* Norwich, VT (Argo Books) 1973, etc. For the Canadian response, see Eugene D. Tate, "The Communication Theorist as Pirate and Argonaut: Eugen Rosenstock-Huessy and Communication Theory," *Canadian Journal of Communication,* Vol. 11, No. 3, Summer 1985, pp. 287-307; and also Eugen D. Tate, "Developments in Communication Theory," *Canadian Journal of Communication,* Vol. 7, No. 3, 1980/81, pp. 58-60.

16. Barrington Nevitt, *The Communication Ecology,* Toronto

(Butterworths) 1982, p. iv, expanding on an earlier, similar formulation by Edward T. Hall.

17. Figure 1 adapted from Gertrude R. Levy, *The Gate of Horn*, London (Faber & Faber) 1948, Plate I(c).

18. B. Nevitt, *The Communication Ecology, op. cit.*, e.g., pp. 176-77.

19. Cf. S. Eastham, *Nucleus, op. cit.*, pp. 39-43.

20. Cf. Ernst Cassirer, *An Essay on Man*, New Haven, CN (Yale University Press) 1944, e.g., Chapter II, "A Clue to the Nature of Man: The Symbol," pp. 25-28.

21. Clifford Geertz, *The Interpretation of Cultures*, New York (Basic Books) 1973, p. 218.

22. Cf., e.g., Lewis Mumford, *The City in History*, New York (Harcourt, Brace & World) 1961; and perhaps more to our point, the early chapters of *Technics and Human Development, op. cit.*

23. For a handy illustrated resumé of these and other Fuller inventions, see R. Buckminster Fuller and R. Marks, *The Dymaxion World of Buckminster Fuller*, New York (Anchor/ Doubleday) 1973.

24. Cf. R. Buckminster Fuller, *Synergetics: Explorations in the Geometry of Thinking*, New York (Macmillan) 1975, 1979, §641.00, p. 357.

25. *Ibid.*, §640.00 sq. Appendix I from §643.00.

26. This derivation of communications theory from the classical *trivium* of rhetoric, grammar and logic (or dialectic) apparently began with Marshall McLuhan's doctoral dissertation, "The Place of Thomas Nashe in the Learning of his Time," University of Cambridge, 1942, and continues as a seemingly self-evident point of departure in Nevitt *(Communication Ecology, op. cit.)* and many another contemporary theorist of communication (e.g., Nancy Harper, *Communication Theory: The History of a Paradigm,* Rochelle Park, NJ (Hayden) 1979). In his *Laws of Media - The New Science,* Toronto (University of Toronto Press) 1988, Eric McLuhan goes some distance toward redressing the compressive thrust I am concerned about, which remains the principle legacy of classical rhetoric. Even in the West, Heraclitus' *logos,* and the *logos* of the New Testament, and the medieval four levels of exegesis are far deeper and broader than mere tips for the propagandist on how to convince an audience. Indeed, by the Middle Ages, it can be said that the Book of God's Works (Nature) and the Book of God's Word (Scripture) had been brought into a consonance utterly lost to the modern mentality. But the monocultural focus of communication studies on western philosophical models remains a tremendous handicap, especially in today's world where the encounter of formerly insular cultures is a social, political and religious imperative. To ignore the entire Indo-European heritage symbolized by *vac* (the feminine Word) in the Hindu *shruti,* to omit the medieval religious intuition of the intra- and extra-trinitarian communication that calls the world into being through the Word, to neglect the reciprocity of sacrifice and

sacrament as the kenotic dynamism of this process for all the Indo-European cultures, to gloss over the Confucian *cheng ming* (rectification of terminology; see my *Paradise & Ezra Pound,* cited below, n. 30), to forget the symbiosis of rhythm (silence, silent intervals) and word in the songs and chants of the shamans -- these lacunae leave much undone, and leave moreover the impression that communication is something people started to do in a critically conscious way only in classical Greece. Presumably a depth immersion in Martin Heidegger's later work on language would be a strong antidote to this bias, or at least a good place to begin re-thinking the entire problematic within the western tradition. Or, one might gain another kind of foothold altogether on the Indo-European heritage by considering the subtleties of Rg Veda I, 164, 34-45 -- "The Word is measured in four *pada* (feet)," etc. -- which may well be the eldest human text on the Word, antedating Greek speculation by about 1,500 years. (Cf. R. Panikkar, *The Vedic Experience,* Berkeley/Los Angeles (University of California Press) 1977, Chapter I.B., "The Word," pp. 88-112.)

27. "How do ideas, information, steps of logical or pragmatic consistency, and the like fit together? How is logic, the classical procedure for making chains of ideas, related to an outside world of things and creatures, parts and wholes? Do ideas really occur in chains, or is this lineal structure imposed on them by scholars and philosophers? How is the world of logic, which eschews 'circular argument,' related to a world in which circular trains of causation are the rule rather than the exception?" Gregory Bateson, *Mind and Nature, op. cit.*, p. 20. Cf. Peter Pearce, *Pattern Is a Design Strategy in Nature,* Boston

(M.I.T. Press) 1979.

28. R. Buckminster Fuller, *Synergetics, op. cit.*, §640.50, p. 356.

29. R. Buckminster Fuller, "The Design Initiative," *World Design Science Decade*, 1965-1975 series, Document #2. See also Anthony Pugh, *An Introduction to Tensegrity,* Berkeley and Los Angeles (University of California Press) 1976.

30. Scott Eastham, *Paradise & Ezra Pound - The Poet as Shaman,* Lanham, MD (University Press of America) 1983.

31. Hugh Kenner, *The Pound Era,* Berkeley/Los Angeles (University of California Press) 1971, p. 168.

32. Dennis Murphy, "Taking Media on their Own Terms: The Integration of the Human and the Technological," in George E. Lasker, Ed., *Advances in Systems Research and Cybernetics,* Windsor (International Institute for Advanced Studies in Systems Research and Cybernetics) 1989. *Pace,* Nevitt, *The Communication Ecology, op. cit.,* Chapter 9, "Grammars of the Media," pp. 125-148.

33. Indeed, as I shall clarify shortly, they might best be considered forms of language.

34. George Steiner's translation (cited) of this passage from "Dichterisch Wohnet der Mensch..." (1954) forms part of the epigraph to his *After Babel - Aspects of Language and Translation,* London (Oxford) 1975, p. xi. Cf. also A. Hofstadter's alternative translation in Martin Heidegger, *Poetry,*

Language, Thought, New York (Harper & Row) 1975, pp. 215-16.

35. "And the Music Never Stopped," Weir/Barlow, *Blues for Allah,* Grateful Dead, Round Records, 1975.

36. Cf. e.g., Aristotle, *Metaphysics,* R. Hope trans., Ann Arbor, MI (University of Michigan Press) 1952, Book XI (Kappa), 5, 1062(a): "...the same thing cannot at one and the same time be and not be, or have any other similar set of opposites." (p. 228)

37. Gregory Bateson, *Mind and Nature, op. cit.,* Chapter III/9, "The Case of 'Description,' 'Tautology,' and 'Explanation,'" pp. 81-88.

38. Why is it the human mind seems to gravitate between monistic and dualistic models of intelligibility? Consider the following schema:

Left lobe, analytic, dualistic;
principle of non-contradiction: A≠B.

> "When looking for an ultimate reality...the way of thinking based mainly on the principle of non-contradiction will obviously look for something different from everyday experience: the Ultimate will then be considered transcendent, wholly Other, superior, difference, cause, mover...and the like. This procedure will lead to the 'God' of the abrahamic religious traditions." *

Right lobe, *Gestalt*, monistic;
principle of identity: A=A.

> "When looking for an ultimate reality, the way of thinking based mainly on the principle of identity will obviously look for something self-identical in our common experience: the Ultimate will then be considered immanent, the real One, basic, intrinsically identical, condition of possibility and the like. This will lead to the Brahman of the indian religious tradition." **

And the balance between these views is presumably what is called sanity.

* R. Panikkar, "Singularity and Individuality. The Double Principle of Individuation," in *Revue Internationale de Philosophie*, 111-112, 1975, fasc. 1-2, pp. 141-166. Quotation from p. 147.

** *Ibid.*

39. Cf., e.g., Roland Barthes, *Elements of Semiology*, London (Cape) 1967.

40. D. Murphy, "Taking Media on Their own Terms," *op. cit., loc. cit.*

41. Cf. Ernst Cassirer, *The Philosophy of Symbolic Forms*, e.g., Vol. 2, *Mythical Thought*, New Haven/London (Yale University

Press) 1955.

42. Cf. Susanne K. Langer, *Philosophy in a New Key*, New York (New American Library) 1951.

43. The bibliography here is enormous. Besides the *Collected Works* of Carl Gustav Jung, cf. Jung, *The Undiscovered Self*, Boston, MA (Atlantic/Little Brown) 1958 and, for a good introduction to this school of thought, Jung et al., *Man and His Symbols*, London (Aldus Books) 1964. Neumann and Hilman are for those with more specialized interests, as are the *Eranos Jahrbucher* documenting their extraordinary annual conferences, but much of this material is skillfully summarized by Joseph Campbell, in, e.g., *The Masks of God*, Vols. I-IV, New York (Vintage) 1959 sq.

44. To appreciate this highly telescoped epigram at its proper depth, cf. the final few chapters of Norman O. Brown, *Love's Body*, New York (Vintage) 1966.

45. Cf. Paul Ricoeur, *The Symbolism of Evil*, New York (Harper & Row) 1967, "Conclusion: The Symbol Gives Rise to Thought," pp. 347-57.

46. Raimundo Panikkar, *Worship and Secular Man*, London (Darton, Longman & Todd) 1973, p. 21.

47. *Ibid.*, p. 20.

48. *Ibid.*, pp. 20-21.

49. Raimundo Panikkar, *Myth, Faith & Hermeneutics,* Ramsey, NJ (Paulist Press) 1979, pp. 6-7. One should note also that the passage cited goes on to describe the symbol as a container: *patra,* jar, vessel: "And it is the function of the sacrifice to break the vessel with which the light is covered. Revelation is this uncovering of the symbol."

50. *Ibid.*, p. 8.

51. Cf. e.g., Robert Logan, *The Alphabet Effect,* New York (Morrow) 1986.

52. H. Marshall McLuhan, *Understanding Media - The Extensions of Man,* New York (McGraw-Hill) 1964, p. 23.

53. In point of fact, he calls it "a symbolist statement," Nevitt, *The Communication Ecology, op. cit.*, p. 146, presumably thereby invoking McLuhan's literary affiliations with the French symbolist poets.

54. Cf. Jonathan Schell, *The Fate of the Earth,* New York (Knopf) 1982, Chapter II, "The Second Death," pp. 97-179.

55. Cf. Derrick de Kerckhove, "On Nuclear Communication," *Diacritics,* Summer 1984, pp. 72-81.

56. *Ibid.*, p. 72.

57. Cf. S. Eastham *Nucleus, op. cit.*, "The Future," pp. 100-118.

58. Ezra Pound, "Affirmations, IV," *The New Age,* 28 January

1915, p. 349.

59. Ezra Pound, "Medievalism," reprinted as "Cavalcanti - Medievalism," in *Literary Essays,* selected and introduced by T. S. Eliot, London (Faber & Faber) 1954; Norfolk, CN (New Directions) 1960, pp. 149-200. Quotation from p. 154 of the latter edition.

60. Appendix II freely adapted from tables appearing in R. Buckminster Fuller, *Critical Path,* New York (St. Martin's Press) 1981 and Lewis Mumford, *Technology and Human Civilization,* New York (Harcourt, Brace & World) 1934.

61. *Aliter,* Chapter 6 (and Fig. 3) below, "the [isotropic vector] matrix."

62. Cf., e.g., Ezra Pound, *Gaudier-Brzeska: A Memoir,* New York (New Directions) 1961, p. 86; and for the fully illuminated demonstration, "Section Rock-Drill, Cantos 85-95" of *The Cantos of Ezra Pound,* New York (New Directions) 1970.

63. Cf. Richard of St. Victor, *The Twelve Patriarchs and The Mystical Ark,* (i.e., *Benjamin Minor & Benjamin Major)* G. A. Zinn trans., Ramsey, NJ (Paulist Press) 1979; e.g., notes on light and ecstasy in Introduction, pp. 19-22.

64. Cf. J. Hillis Miller, *Poets of Reality,* Cambridge, MA. (Harvard University Press) 1965, "The Poetry of Reality," pp. 1-12.

65. The threshold of intelligibility shifts. In his *Laws of*

Media, op. cit., Eric McLuhan distinguishes between human artifacts (to which his "laws" apply) and all natural processes (to which they do not). Gregory Bateson in *Mind and Nature, op. cit.,* finds natural analogues to human language in all biological life *(creatura),* while he finds no such correlates in the world of physics *(pleroma).* A poet, however, discerns a wider horizon of intelligibility, as does Ezra Pound in *The Spirit of Romance,* New York (New Directions) 1952, pp. 92-93:

> "Our kinship to the ox we have constantly thrust upon us; but beneath this is our kinship to the vital universe, to the tree and the living rock, and, because this is less obvious -- and possibly more interesting -- we forget it.
>
> "We have about us the universe of fluid force, and below us the germinal universe of wood alive, of stone alive....and the strength of the Greek beauty rests in this, that it is ever at the interpretation of this vital universe, by its signs of gods and godly attendants and oreads."

66. Cf. "Tradition and the Individual Talent," Thomas Stearns Eliot, *Selected Essays,* New York (Harcourt, Brace & Co.), 1932, 1936, 1950, pp. 3-11. I might add that in the 'tradition' of academic papers, it is often mainly the *notes* that trace the tensile continuities (or ricocheting divergences) of the present work to or from its own context.

67. Cf. Thomas Eric Mars McLuhan, *Menippean Thunder at*

"Finnegans Wake": The Critical Problems, Ann Arbor, MI (University Microfilms International) 1983.

68. James Joyce, *Finnegans Wake,* New York (Viking) 1967, p. 497.

69. Cf. H. Marshall McLuhan, *The Letters of Marshall McLuhan,* M. Molinaro, C. McLuhan and W. Toye, Ed., Toronto (Oxford) 1987.

70. Ernest Fenollosa, *The Chinese Written Character as a Medium for Poetry,* E. Pound, Ed., San Francisco (City Lights) 1969, p. 12.

71. *Ibid.,* pp. 10, 13.

72. *Ibid.,* p. 22.

73. Cf. S. Eastham, *Nucleus, op. cit.,* pp. 79-81.

74. Neils Bohr, *Atomic Physics and the Description of Nature,* London (Cambridge University Press) 1934, p. 96.

75. William Carlos Williams, *Spring & All* (1923), Frontier Press reprint, 1970, p. 80.

76. "These fragments I have shored against my ruins," line 430, T. S. Eliot, *The Wasteland* (Facsimile Edition, V. Eliot, Ed.), New York (Harvest Books) 1971, pp. 88, 89, 146.

77. Cf. Jan C. Smuts, *Holism and Evolution,* New York (Macmil-

lan) 1926, particularly Chapter V, "General Concept of Holism."

78. Cf. José Ortega y Gasset, *What is Philosophy?*, M. Adams, trans., New York (Norton) 1960, especially Chapters 9 & 10. Cf. also Martin Heidegger, *Being and Time*, J. Macquarrie & E. Robinson, trans., New York (Harper & Row) 1962, notably Part One, Division One, Chapter II, "Being-in-the-world in General as the Basic State of Dasein," e.g., p. 80: *"'Being-in' is thus the formal existential expression for the Being of Dasein, which has Being-in-the-world as its essential state."*

79. Marshall McLuhan called him "The Leonardo da Vinci of our time." (Cited on video cover note, Robert Snyder, *The World of Buckminster Fuller*, Masters & Masterworks, Pacific Palisades, CA.)

80. R. Buckminster Fuller, *Synergetics, op. cit.*, §301.10 Definition: Universe (1975 formulation), p. 81.

81. Ralph Waldo Emerson, *The Works of Ralph Waldo Emerson*, New York (Tudor) "Shakespeare; or, The Poet," (1850), p. 246.

82. This is vintage Fuller, of course (cf. *Synergetics, op. cit.*, for Fuller's very specific use of the term "frequency," e.g., §413.04, 505.03, 1054.70-72, Figs. 516.03, C&D, etc.), but it is also a way of restating Planck's radiation law, that everything is a frequency, a multiple of h (Plank's constant for a unit quantum of energy: $h = 6.6 \times 10^{-27}$ grams cm^2/sec.).

83. H. Marshall McLuhan, *Letters, op. cit.*, p. 448.

84. "Only a limit enables a form to rise to perfection," as Johann Wolfgang von Goethe wrote in "Metamorphosis of Animals" (1806), *Selected Poems,* C. Middleton, Ed., London (Calder) 1983, p. 161. Cf. likewise, composer Gian Carlo Menotti's recent description of Mozart's technique in his essay "I Forgive Goethe, Tolstoy and, Above All, Mozart," *The New York Times,* 10 June 1989: "What moves one is not only the beauty of his melodic line (undoubtedly a God-given gift) but the intellectual skill with which he handles it, bends it to his will, and the severity with which he imprisons it into the most restrictive classical tradition. He does not ask for freedom as most artists do today. On the contrary, he uses such restrictions as a challenge, an intricate puzzle to be solved by careful thought."

85. E. Pound, *Spirit of Romance, op. cit.,* p. 97. Ohm's Law, conventionally stated: The strength or intensity of an unvarying electrical current (DC) is directly proportional to the electromotive force (voltage), and inversely proportional to the resistance of the circuit: $i=v/r$.

86. H. Marshall McLuhan, *Understanding Media, op. cit.,* pp. 70-71.

87. Cf. Brian Fawcett, *Cambodia -- a book for people who find television too slow,* Vancouver, BC (Talonbooks) 1986.

88. Keith Jarrett, *Standards* -- Jarrett, piano; Gary Peacock, bass; Jack DeJohnette, drums -- a February 1985 concert in Tokyo's Koseinenkin Hall consisting solely of jazz standards from the 30's, 40's and 50's... something of a departure for

these gentlemen.

89. Cf. John Fowles, *The French Lieutenant's Woman*, New York (Little, Brown) 1969, particularly Chapter 13, where the tension established by this procedure suddenly flips around like a snapped rubber band; and also John Fowles, *A Maggot*, New York (Little, Brown) 1985.

90. E. McLuhan, *Laws of Media, op. cit.*, p. 100. *(Pace*, H. M. McLuhan and W. Walker, *From Cliché to Archetype*, New York (Viking) 1970.)

91. *Ibid.*, especially Chapters 3 & 4. It may be that enhancement and obsolescence are the compressive ('establishment') forces at work in the artifacts McLuhan examines, while retrieval and reversal represent the tensional ('resistance') elements. Eric McLuhan claims not to perceive these 'diagonals' at work in his tetrads, but couldn't resist delivering himself of an apt acoustic pun upon the topic after reading a draft of this chapter: "Ohm is where the Art is."

92. Cf. Scott Eastham, "'*by defective means --*' Poetic Diction and Divine Apparition in William Carlos Williams' Later Poetry," *Sagetrieb*, Vol. 5, No. 1, Spring 1986, pp. 17-27.

93. Wyndham Lewis's *BLAST* (London, 1914) carried a short piece by Ezra Pound on Laurence Binyon, in which he cited these passages from Binyon's *Flight of the Dragon*, pp. 19, 21. In the Introduction to his Cavalcanti translations (Ezra Pound, *Translations*, New York (New Directions) 1963), Pound also wrote (p. 23), "I believe in an ultimate and absolute rhythm,"

emphasizing as always that the emotional continuities of a poem were given in the cadence, the resonant intervals, the tensional embrace. Cf. Scott Eastham, "Hear/Say - Ezra Pound and the Ten Voices of Tradition," *Rendezvous*, Ezra Pound Centennial Edition, Vol. XXII, No. 1, Fall, 1986, pp. 8-25, for further exploration of the dimension of acoustic interiority in Pound's poetry.

94. Cf. Jean Baudrillard, *Simulations,* New York (Semiotext(e)) 1983, particularly the first essay, "The Precession of Simulacra," a powerful critique of the rampant modern tendency for the model (icon) to run ahead of the phenomenon, until there is no "satz" but only "ersatz," no reality but only "hyperreality."

95. Here and elsewhere in the next few pages I am drawing from and would like to refer the reader to the synergetics primer I co-authored some time ago with Mr. John Blackman, *Unfolding Wholes - R. Buckminster Fuller & The Sacred Geometry of Nature*, but the book has unfortunately not yet found a publisher willing to produce the 'four-dimensional' models which accompany it. It's not easy to launch a round thing in a square world...

96. In Martin Heidegger, *Identity and Difference*, New York (Harper & Row) 1969, translator Joan Stambaugh provides the following exegesis of Heidegger's word *Gestell,* which is generally translated "frame" or "framework." It has very many resonances in German which do not quite carry over into the English:

"*'Ge-stell'* in the sense in which Heidegger uses it

> does not belong to common language. In German, '*Berg*' means a mountain, '*Gebirge*' means a chain or a group of mountains. In the same way, '*Ge-stell*' is the unity (but *not* a unity in the sense of a general whole subsuming all particulars under it) of all the activities in which the verb '*stellen*' (place, put, set) figures: *vor-stellen* (represent, think), *stellen* (challenge), *ent-stellen* (disfigure), *nach-stellen* (to be after someone, pursue him stealthily) *sicher-stellen* (to make certain of something)." (p. 14)

97. *Ibid.*, pp. 34-5.

98. Cf. Martin Heidegger, *The Question Concerning Technology,* W. Lovitt, trans., New York (Harper & Row) 1977, especially the two essays comprising Part III, "The Age of the World Picture" and "Science and Reflection."

99. Cf., e.g., H. Marshall McLuhan, *The Gutenberg Galaxy,* Toronto (University of Toronto Press) 1962; José Argüelles, *The Transformative Vision,* Boulder, CO (Shambhala) 1975; Samuel Y. Edgerton, Jr., *The Renaissance Rediscovery of Linear Perspective,* New York (Harper & Row) 1976.

100. R. Buckminster Fuller, *Utopia or Oblivion,* New York (Overlook Press) 1969, p. 76:

> "In 1917, I found myself asserting that I didn't think nature had a department of chemistry, a department of mathematics, a department of physics, and a department of biology and had to have meetings of

department heads in order to decide what to do when you drop your stone in the water. Universe, i.e. nature, obviously knows just what to do, and everything seemed beautifully coordinate. The lily pads did just what they should do, and the fish did just what they should do. Everything went sublimely, smoothly. So I thought that nature probably had one coordinate system and probably one most economical arithmetical and geometric system with which to interaccount all transactions and transformations. And I thought also that it was preposterous when I was told that real models are not employed in advanced science, because science was able to deal with nature by use of completely unmodelable mathematical abstractions. I could not credit that universe suddenly went abstract at some micro-level of investigation, wherefore you had to deal entirely with abstract-formula, unmodelable mathematics... I thought then that if we could find nature's own coordinate system we would understand the models and would be able to develop much higher exploratory and application capability. I felt that if we ever found nature's coordinate system, it would be very simple and always rational."*

* By "rational" here, Fuller means "in whole-number increments."

101. G. Bateson, *Mind and Nature, op. cit.*, p. 17.

102. R. B. Fuller, *Synergetics, op. cit.;* Figure 3 is Fig. 420.02, p.

139; Figure 4 is from Fig. 413.01, p. 118. Cf. also Amy C. Edmonson, *A Fuller Explanation - The Synergetic Geometry of R. Buckminster Fuller,* Cambridge, MA (Birkhauser Boston) 1987, Chapters 7-9. Edmonson's recent book is the most comprehensive available exposition of Fuller's geometry other than *Synergetics* itself and, from this layman's perspective at least, a model of mathematical clarity.

103. Hugh Kenner, *Bucky - A Guided Tour of Buckminster Fuller,* New York (Morrow) 1973, out of print but still the most readable introduction to Fuller's life and thought. Cf. Kenner's versions of Figures 3 and 4 on pp. 109-110.

104. Cf. the article first announcing "Buckminsterfullerene" (C_{60}) in *Nature,* Vol. 318, No. 6042, November 1985.

105. R. B. Fuller, *Synergetics, op. cit.,* §440.00, "Zero Model," p. 156.

106. B. Nevitt, *Communication Ecology, op. cit.,* p. 38.

107. Cited in H. Kenner, *Bucky, op. cit.,* p. 116, and also spoken by Fuller himself in R. Snyder's film, *The World of Buckminster Fuller, op. cit.* The full quotation:

> "The vector equilibrium contains the whole phenomenology of the universe. The vector equilibrium is never witnessed by man. It is as pure as God. It is truth which is approached; it is exactitude that is approached."

108. As a single example, I recently came across one of the earliest instances of 60° radial symmetry in a striking Harrapan bas relief found on the walls of Mohenjo Daro in the Indus Valley, dating back at least 4,000 years. The resemblance to Fuller's geometry is so exact that the black Vector Equilibrium 'disk' presented in Appendix IV might almost be a rubbing taken from that venerable carving. Besides later serving as the graphic figure for the second (genital, generative) chakra -- described in the literature as "energy's own standing space" -- and as the model for innumerable common yantras (meditation diagrams), its circular 60° symmetry may well have provided a prototype for the six-fold architectural symmetry of many later Hindu temples. This is not the place to detail the myriad further correspondences with the Minoan *labrys,* or the Pythagorean *tetraktys,* or Celtic knots, or cathedral rose windows, but these pre-Cartesian crystallizations of the isotropic vector matrix and its characteristic 60° symmetry are undeniably tangled up with the very roots of Indo-European culture. And, not altogether surprisingly, with those of very many other cultures as well... Indeed, once you start looking for Nature's coordinate system in the iconographies and sacred geometries of traditional cultures, you can scarcely avoid discovering antecedents everywhere.

109. Development is of course more often the problem than the solution. A growing chorus of scholars are seeking alternatives; cf., e.g., *Alternatives au développement,* R. Vachon, Ed., Montreal (Centre Interculturel Monchanin) 1988. Cf. also the recent works of Illich, Sachs, Esteva, et al.

110. Cf. R. B. Fuller, *Synergetics, op. cit.,* §610.00 "Triangulation." Cf. also Appendix III, ∆.

111. For two disparate examples, cf. Sr. Prudence Allen, "Synergetics and Sex Complementarity," a paper affirming the "asymmetrical complementarity" of the sexes, presented at the World Congress of Philosophy in Brighton, England, August 1988, and also Marion Mona Odell Carr, *The Discovery and Application of Synergetic Tetrahedral Communication Models,* Philadelphia, PA (Temple University Ph.D. Dissertation) 1979, which sounds promising, although I have unfortunately not been able to obtain a copy before this book goes to press.

112. Cf. R. Panikkar, "The Myth of Pluralism: The Tower of Babel - A Meditation on Nonviolence," in *Cross Currents,* No. XXIX, No. 2, Summer 1979, pp. 197-230.

113. This is in principle the resolution proposed by G. Bateson to the title thematic of his *Mind and Nature, op. cit.;* both are stochastic systems: "If a sequence of events combines a random component with a selective process so that only certain outcomes of the random are allowed to endure, that sequence is said to be *stochastic.*" (p. 230)

114. Cf., e.g., Arthur Koestler, *Janus - A Summing Up,* New York (Vintage/Random House) 1978.

115. Cf., e.g., the "implicate order" of physicist David Bohm, *Wholeness and the Implicate Order,* London (Routledge & Kegan Paul) 1980, and the "morphogenetic field" of Rupert

Sheldrake, *A New Science of Life*, Los Angeles (Tarcher) 1981, or "the greatest membrane" in Lewis Thomas, *Lives of a Cell*, New York (Viking) 1974, as well as the immanent divinity or "Goddess" of New Age witches like Starhawk, *The Spiral Dance*, New York (Harper & Row) 1980.

116. Cf., e.g., S. Eastham, *Nucleus, op. cit.*, "The Secular as Sacred," pp. 25-38, the discussion of *anima mundi*, pp. 94-99, and "The Goddess Aroused," pp. 179-181.

117. E. Pound, *The Cantos, op. cit.*, Canto 87, p. 573.

118. N. O. Brown, *Love's Body, op. cit.*, p. 266. Here Brown is conflating two famous aphorisms into a memorable one of his own. First there is Johann Wolfgang von Goethe's "Alles Vergängliche is nur ein Gleichnis" (Everything transitory is but a metaphor), *Faust* II. 5. 12104-5; then Friedrich Nietzsche's retort, "Alles Unvergängliche is nur ein Gleichnis" (Everything eternal is but a metaphor). Same difference?

###

Appendix I - **Tension & Compression: Summary***

Compression is IN.	*Tension* is OUT.
Compression is dispersive both laterally and circumferentially, inherently electrostatic because differentiative divisive, temporary and local.	*Tension* is omniradially conversive and is both electromagnetically and gravitationally tensive because eternally comprehensive.
Compression tends to local dichotomy and multiplication by separation.	*Tension* is unit: universally cohering and comprehensively finite. [...]
Compression accumulates potential. As demonstrated in the arch, compression is limited to absolute, local, and within-law relationships of one fixed system.	*Tension* is comprehensive, attractive, and gravitational. Tension is inherently integral and eternally, invisibly, infinitely comprehensive. Tension is comprehensively without-law.
Compression tends toward arcs of decreasing radius.	*Tension* tends toward arcs of increasing radius.
Compressions are plural.	*Tension* is singular.
Compression is time.	*Tension* is eternity.
Compression is specifically directional.	*Tension* is both omni- and supra-directional.
Compression is inherently partial.	*Tension* is inherently total.

(*R. B. Fuller, *Synergetics* §643)

Appendix II

Reconnoitering The Electromagnetic Universe

Freely adapted from chronological tables in R. B. Fuller's *Critical Path* and L. Mumford's *Technology & Human Civilization.*

- 1864 - Electromagnetic Theory - Maxwell

- 1877 - Phonograph - Edison
  Series photography - Muybridge
  Chronophotographic gun - Marey

- 1878 - Incandescent Lamp - Edison
  Cathode Ray - Crooks

- 1887 - Automatic Telephone - Bell
  Electromagnetic Waves - Hertz

- 1889 - Kinetograph, first true motion picture camera - Edison Labs, NJ

- 1895 - Wireless Telegraphy
  X-Ray - Roentgen
  Cinematographe - Lumière Bros

- 1896 - Radioactive Emissions of Uranium - Becquerel

- 1897 - Radio Tuning - Lodge
  Electron - J. J. Thompson

- 1901 - Transatlantic Radio Telegraph - Marconi; filling the ether with patterns.

The Media Matrix

- 1902 - Radio Telegram
  Photos by wire

- 1903 - Pacific cable; message around the world
  in 12 minutes.

- 1906 - $E = mc^2$ - Special Theory of Relativity -
  Einstein

- 1908 - Electron confirmed - Millikan.
  Genetic Patterns - Mendel

- 1910 - Continuous wave radio transmission -
  Poulson

- 1911 - Recognition of protons
  X-ray study of metals
  Cloud chamber
  Kinemacolor movies

- 1912 - X-ray spectra, X-ray crystallography
  Atomic Nucleus - Moseley

- 1913 - Tungsten filament lamp
  Research on radiation - Geiger
  Atomic 'solar system' model - Bohr

- 1915 - Transcontinental phone service
  High vacuum radio tube - Langmuir
  Tuned radio frequency reception -
  Alexanderson
  Einstein's General Theory of Relativity
  Radiotelephone

The Media Matrix

- 1919 - First wireless phone call; two-way transatlantic conversation

- 1920 - Commercial radio broadcast of voice.

- 1922 - AC radio tube
  Radar

- 1924 - Complementarity - Bohr

- 1926 - Talking movies
  The Wasteland, T.S. Eliot
  A Draft of XVI Cantos, Ezra Pound

- 1927 - Television, in laboratory only - Farnsworth, Zworykin
  Heisenberg's Indeterminacy
  Photoelectric cell
  Michaelson's final, most accurate measurement of speed of light in vacuum
  Ulysses, James Joyce
  Holism & Evolution, J. Smuts
  Sein und Zeit, M. Heidegger

###

Appendix III - Triangle

In order to forestall misunderstanding, it is perhaps necessary to note that 'triangle' is not the closed, static entity which Euclid and his schoolmarm minions would have us believe, and which has given geometry as a whole a bad reputation for rigidity. Fuller's geometry of energy and synergy disputes Euclid's most fundamental axioms directly. For Fuller, and for modern physics as well, there are no points, no lines, no planes, no solids, or any of the other staples of planar geometry. He demonstrates that triangle is actually a threefold vector diagram of an energy event:

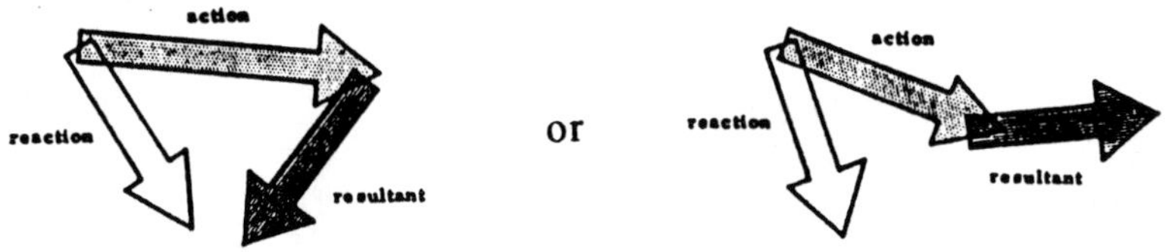

The way of the triangle is to spiral. Triangles are really spirals. That third angle is always open (even if ever so slightly) -- to other events, other configurations and constellations of energy.

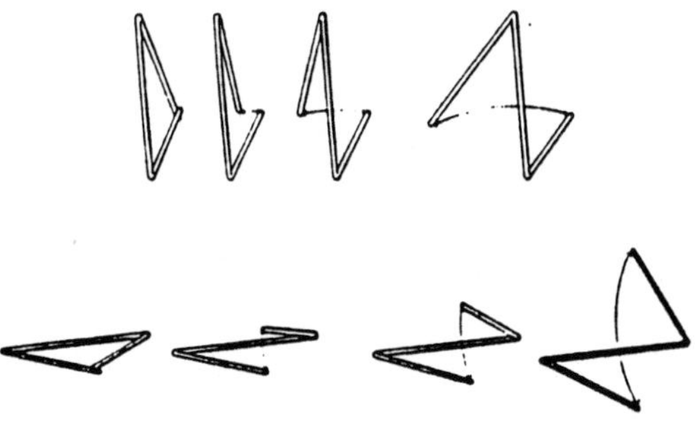

There is no volume, no depth dimension contained, until two such events come together -- and mate, so speak, to form a tetrahedron.

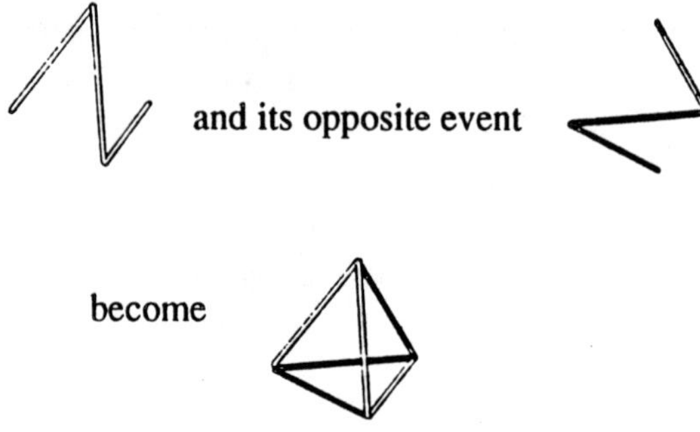

Or, as Fuller would have it it: **1 + 1 = 4.**

###

Appendix IV - Spherical Vector Equilibrium: One WHOLE Kit

There is a severe problem with this little book, namely, that it cannot be illustrated properly in the two dimensions permitted by the printed page. At least one geodesic illustration is therefore in order.

WHOLES are the models par excellence of electromagnetic wave phenomena, spherical wave growth out from centers (nuclei). They are tensegrity structures which chart, in a very striking way, the relationship between center and circumference. The great-circles of paper form the tensional continuum, while the pins are the discontinuous compressives.

R. Buckminster Fuller first published the specifications for seven of these 'great-circle' models in *Synergetics* -- §450.10, 455.11, 458.12 -- and soon thereafter gave his permission for them to be christened WHOLES (pun intended). The spherical vector equilibrium is the simplest of such geodesic sculptures, utilizing only four disks of paper and twelve pins (bobby pins or light gauge cotter pins will do the job). Fuller described the surprising behavior of such figures as follows:

"It is characteristic of electromagnetic wave phenomena that a wave must return upon itself, completing a 360-degree circuit. The great circle disks folded or flat provide unitary wave-cycle circumferential circuits. Therefore, folded or not, they act like waves coming back upon themselves in a perfect wave control. We find their precessional cyclic self-interferences producing angular resultants that shunt themselves into little local 60-degree bow-tie 'holding patterns.' The entire behavior is characteristic of generalized wave phenomena."

Unfolding the Vector Equilibrium

MATERIALS: 4 disks scored at 60° angles; 12 bobby (or cotter) pins.

WHOLES are made from scored disks which resemble bow-ties when folded and pinned. The 'bow-ties' are then pinned together to form a geodesic sphere.

TO FORM THE BOW-TIES:

1) Fold each disk in half along each diameter as shown in Figure 1. (Make sharp creases.)

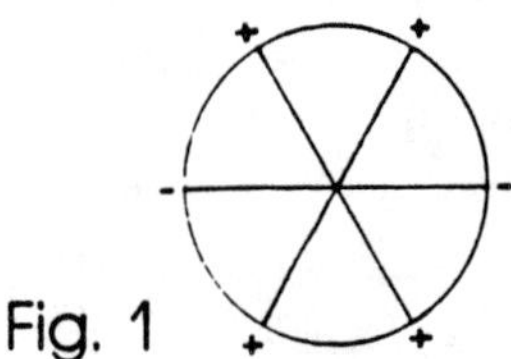

Fig. 1

- = fold AWAY from you

+ = fold TOWARD you

2) Pin each bow-tie as shown in Figure 2.

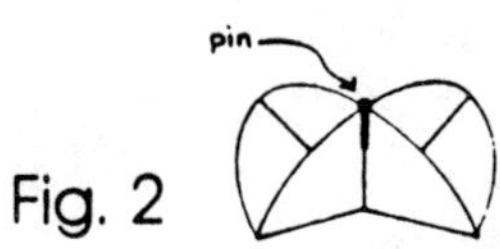

Fig. 2

TO FORM THE SPHERE:

3) Pin the first two bow-ties together as shown in Figure 3.

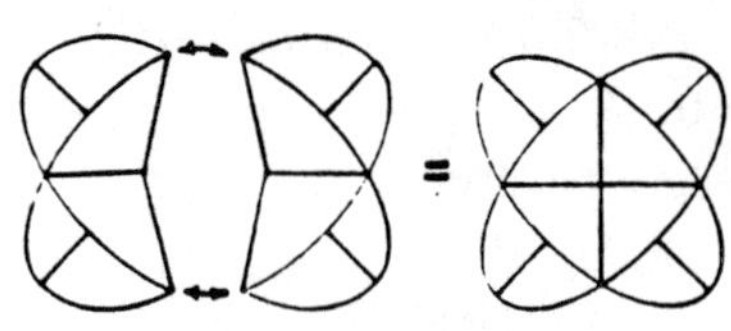

Fig. 3

4) Continue this pattern to pin the remaining bow-ties. Figure 4 shows the complete sphere with one bow-tie in relief.

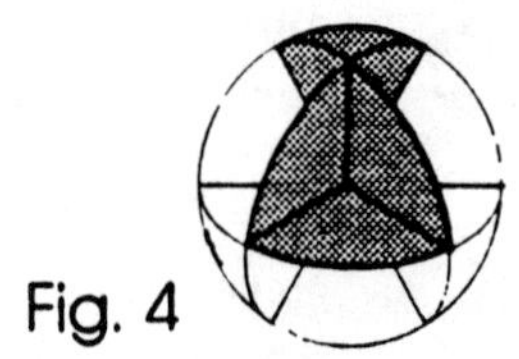
Fig. 4

NOTE: You can expect the bow-ties to slip a little as you pin them, but the figure will adjust itself with the last pin or two. Pinch firmly on the bow-ties to place the last few pins.

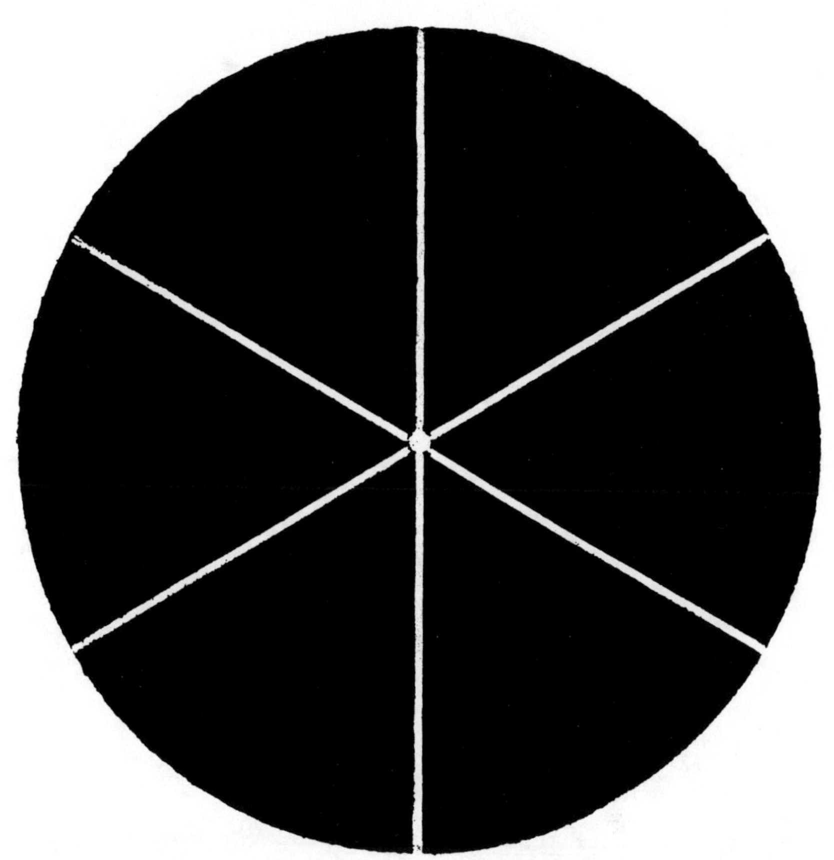

SUGGESTION: The best way to dramatize the alternating tetrahedra and octahedra in your vector equilibrium is to use 'duplex' cover-stock or (lightweight) matte board for the disks. Such 'two-faced' papers are usually white on one side with a primary color on the other. You may simulate the effect with ordinary construction paper by making a black disk like the one above, and scoring with a china white pencil. Then simply photocopy the disk four times for each model.

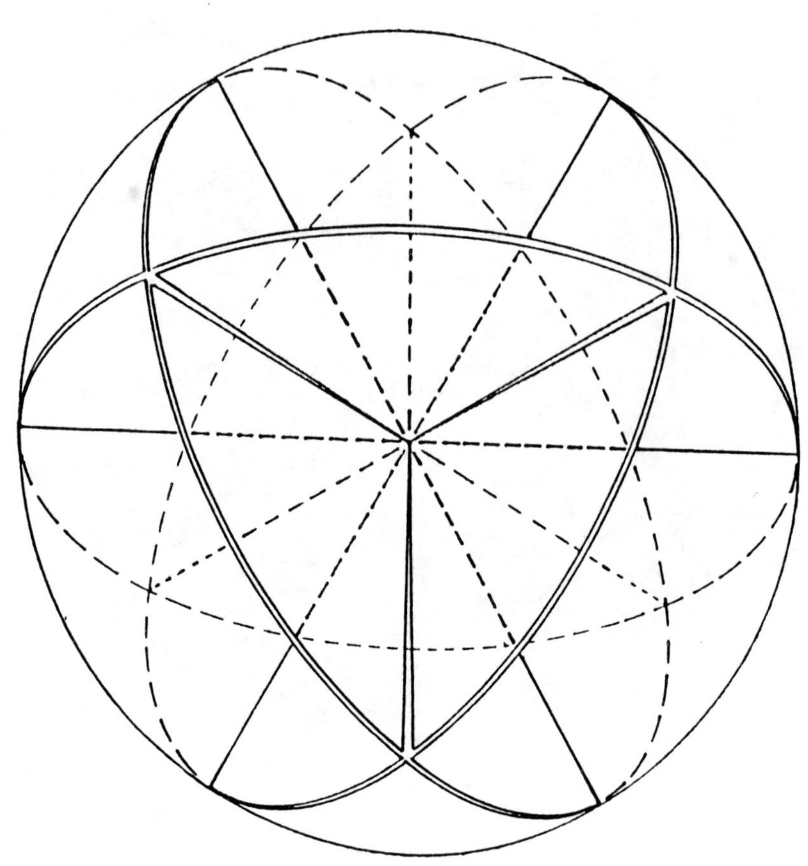

SPHERICAL VECTOR EQUILIBRIUM
Rendered by Tom Parker

Appendix V - Toward A Nondual Epistemology

1	2	3 (or Zero)
MONISTIC	DUALISTIC	NONDUALISTIC
heteronomy	autonomy	ontonomy/holism
other-directed	self-directed	un-self-centered
order	randomness	organism
closed system	open system	stochastic system
pattern	variation	rhythm/music
collectivity	individual	person/community
compulsion	competition	co-evolution
authority	liberty	freedom
tradition	progress	(organic) growth
stability	energy	synergy
being	becoming	life

In the first column, it's the one **or** the many, so that the one always 'wins.' In the second column, it's the one **and** the many, so that the many proliferate and predominate. In the third column, which ought by rights to be in the middle, it's **neither** one nor many, so that the tensile polarity is maintained: *neti, neti.* Note also the enantiadromia, the tendency for these 'opposite' terms to turn into one another when pushed to extremes: the totalitarian regime 'creates' the revolutionaries by repressive measures; and, once in power, the revolutionary council soon becomes the new dictatorship: yin and yang, as it were, each containing the seed of its contrary.

BIBLIOGRAPHY

Allen, Sr. Prudence, "Synergetics and Sex Complementarity," unpublished paper presented at the World Congress of Philosophy in Brighton, England, August 1988 (Copies available from Department of Philosophy, Concordia University, Montréal, Québec.)

Argüelles, José, *The Transformative Vision,* Boulder (Shambhala) 1975

Aristotle, *Metaphysics,* R. Hope trans., Ann Arbor (University of Michigan Press) 1952

Barthes, Roland, *Elements of Semiology,* London (Cape) 1967

Bateson, Gregory, *Mind and Nature - A Necessary Unity,* New York (Dutton) 1979

Baudrillard, Jean, *Simulations,* New York (Semiotext(e)) 1983

Beckett, Samuel, *Waiting for Godot,* New York (Grove) 1954

Bohm, David, *Wholeness and the Implicate Order,* London (Routledge & Kegan Paul) 1980

Bohr, Neils, *Atomic Physics and the Description of Nature,* London (Cambridge University Press) 1934

Brown, Norman O., *Love's Body,* New York (Vintage) 1966

Burke, Kenneth, *Language as Symbolic Action,* Berkeley, CA (University of California Press) 1968

Campbell, Joseph, *The Masks of God,* Vols. I-IV, New York (Vintage) 1959 sq.

Carr, Marion Mona Odell, *The Discovery and Application of Synergetic Tetrahedral Communication Models,* Philadelphia, PA (Temple University Ph.D. Dissertation) 1979 (Copies available from University Microfilms International, Ann Arbor, MI.)

Cassirer, Ernst, *An Essay on Man,* New Haven, CN (Yale University Press) 1944

Cassirer, Ernst, *The Philosophy of Symbolic Forms,* Vol. 2, *Mythical Thought,* New Haven/London (Yale University Press) 1955

Dudek, Louis, *Collected Poetry,* Montréal (Delta Canada) 1971

Eastham, Scott, *Paradise & Ezra Pound - The Poet as Shaman,* Lanham, MD (University Press of America) 1983

Eastham, Scott, "*'by defective means --'* Poetic Diction and Divine Apparition in William Carlos Williams' Later Poetry," *Sagetrieb,* Vol. 5, No. 1, Spring 1986, pp. 17-27

Eastham, Scott, "Hear/Say - Ezra Pound and the Ten Voices of Tradition," *Rendezvous,* Ezra Pound Centennial Edition, Vol. XXII, No. 1, Fall, 1986, pp. 8-25

Eastham, Scott, *Nucleus - Reconnecting Science & Religion in the Nuclear Age,* Santa Fe (Bear & Company) 1987

Eastham, Scott & Blackman, John, *Unfolding Wholes - R.*

Buckminster Fuller & The Sacred Geometry of Nature, unpublished manuscript

Edgerton, Samuel Y., Jr., *The Renaissance Rediscovery of Linear Perspective,* New York (Harper & Row) 1976

Edmonson, Amy C., *A Fuller Explanation - The Synergetic Geometry of R. Buckminster Fuller,* Cambridge, MA (Birkhauser Boston) 1987

Eliot, T. S., *The Wasteland,* (Facsimile Edition, V. Eliot, Ed.), New York (Harvest Books) 1971

Eliot, T. S., *Selected Essays,* New York (Harcourt, Brace & Co.) 1950

Emerson, Ralph Waldo, *The Works of Ralph Waldo Emerson,* New York (Tudor) 1930

Fawcett, Brian, *Cambodia,* Vancouver, BC (Talonbooks) 1986

Fenollosa, Ernest, *The Chinese Written Character as a Medium for Poetry,* E. Pound, Ed., San Francisco (City Lights) 1969

Fowles, John, *The French Lieutenant's Woman,* New York (Little, Brown) 1969

Fowles, John, *A Maggot,* New York (Little, Brown) 1985

Fuller, R. Buckminster, "The Design Initiative," *World Design Science Decade*, 1965-1975 series, Document #2

Fuller, R. Buckminster, *Utopia or Oblivion,* New York

(Overlook Press) 1969

Fuller R. Buckminster, and Marks, R. *The Dymaxion World of Buckminster Fuller*, New York (Anchor/Doubleday) 1973

Fuller, R. Buckminster, and Applewhite, E. J., *Synergetics: Explorations in the Geometry of Thinking*, New York (Macmillan) 1975, 1979

Fuller, R. Buckminster, *Critical Path*, New York (St. Martin's Press) 1981

Gadamer, Hans-Georg, *Truth and Method*, New York (Seabury) 1972

Geertz, Clifford, *The Interpretation of Cultures*, New York (Basic Books) 1973

von Goethe, Johann Wolfgang, *Faust*, C. Hamlin, trans., W. Arnt, Ed., New York (Norton) 1976

von Goethe, Johann Wolfgang, *Selected Poems*, C. Middleton, Ed., London (Calder) 1983

Harper, Nancy, *Communication Theory: History of a Paradigm*, Rochelle Park, NJ (Hayden) 1979

Heidegger, Martin, *Being and Time*, J. Macquarrie & E. Robinson, trans., New York (Harper & Row) 1962

Heidegger, Martin, *Identity and Difference*, J. Stambaugh, trans., New York (Harper & Row) 1969

Heidegger, Martin, *Poetry, Language, Thought,* A. Hofstadter, trans., New York (Harper & Row) 1975

Heidegger, Martin, *The Question Concerning Technology,* W. Lovitt, trans., New York (Harper & Row) 1977

Hewes, Gordon W., "An Explicit Formulation of the Relationship Between Tool-Using, Tool-Making, and the Emergence of Language," *Visible Language,* Vol. VII, No. 2, Spring, 1973, pp. 101-117

Joyce, James, *Finnegans Wake,* New York (Viking) 1967

Jung, Carl Gustav, *The Undiscovered Self,* Boston, MA (Atlantic/Little Brown) 1958

Jung, Carl Gustav, et al., *Man and His Symbols,* London (Aldus Books) 1964

Kenner, Hugh, *The Pound Era,* Berkeley/Los Angeles (University of California Press) 1971

Kenner, Hugh, *Bucky - A Guided Tour of Buckminster Fuller,* New York (Morrow) 1973

de Kerckhove, Derrick, "On Nuclear Communication," *Diacritics,* Summer 1984, pp. 72-81

Koestler, Arthur, *Janus - A Summing Up,* New York (Vintage/Random House) 1978

Langer, Susanne K., *Philosophy in a New Key,* New York (New American Library) 1951

Levy, Gertrude R., *The Gate of Horn*, London (Faber & Faber) 1948

Lewis, Wyndham, *BLAST* (London) 1914

Logan, Robert, *The Alphabet Effect*, New York (Morrow) 1986

Lonergan, Bernard, *Method in Theology*, New York (Herder & Herder) 1972

McLuhan, Eric, *Laws of Media - The New Science*, Toronto (University of Toronto Press) 1988

McLuhan, Thomas Eric Mars, *Menippean Thunder at "Finnegans Wake": The Critical Problems*, Ann Arbor (University Microfilms International) 1983

McLuhan, Herbert Marshall, *The Place of Thomas Nashe in the Learning of his Time*, doctoral dissertation, University of Cambridge, 1942

McLuhan, H. Marshall, *The Gutenberg Galaxy*, Toronto (University of Toronto Press) 1962

McLuhan, H. Marshall, *Understanding Media - The Extensions of Man*, New York (McGraw-Hill) 1964

McLuhan, H. Marshall, and Walker, W., *From Cliché to Archetype*, New York (Viking) 1970

McLuhan, H. Marshall, *The Letters of Marshall McLuhan*, M. Molinaro, C. McLuhan and W. Toye, Ed., Toronto (Oxford) 1987

Menotti, Gian Carlo, "I Forgive Goethe, Tolstoy and, Above All, Mozart," *The New York Times*, 10 June 1989

Miller, J. Hillis, *Poets of Reality*, Cambridge, MA. (Harvard University Press) 1965

Mumford, Lewis, *Technology and Human Civilization*, New York (Harcourt, Brace & World) 1934

Mumford, Lewis, *The City in History*, New York (Harcourt, Brace & World) 1961

Mumford, Lewis, *The Myth of the Machine*, Vol. 1, *Technics and Human Development*, New York (Harcourt, Brace, Jovanovich) 1967

Mumford, Lewis, *My Works and Days*, New York (Harcourt, Brace, Jovanovich) 1979

Murphy, Dennis, "Taking Media on their Own Terms: The Integration of the Human and the Technological," in George E. Lasker, Ed., *Advances in Systems Research and Cybernetics*, Windsor (International Institute for Advanced Studies in Systems Research and Cybernetics) 1989

Nevitt, Barrington, *The Communication Ecology*, Toronto (Butterworths) 1982

Ortega y Gasset, José, *What is Philosophy?*, M. Adams, trans., New York (Norton) 1960

Panikkar, Raimundo, *Worship and Secular Man*, London (Darton, Longman & Todd) 1973

Panikkar, Raimundo, "Singularity and Individuality. The Double Principle of Individuation," *Revue Internationale de Philosophie,* 111-112, 1975, fasc. 1-2, pp. 141-166

Panikkar, Raimundo, *The Vedic Experience,* Berkeley/Los Angeles (University of California Press) 1977

Panikkar, Raimundo, *Myth, Faith & Hermeneutics,* Ramsey, NJ (Paulist Press) 1979

Panikkar, Raimundo, "The Myth of Pluralism: The Tower of Babel - A Meditation on Nonviolence," in *Cross Currents,* No. XXIX, No. 2, Summer 1979, pp. 197-230

Pearce, Peter, *Pattern Is a Design Strategy in Nature,* Boston (M. I. T. Press) 1979

Pound, Ezra, "Affirmations, IV," *The New Age,* 28 January 1915

Pound, Ezra, *The Spirit of Romance,* New York (New Directions) 1952

Pound, Ezra, *Literary Essays,* selected and introduced by T. S. Eliot, London (Faber & Faber) 1954; Norfolk, CN (New Directions) 1960

Pound, Ezra, *Gaudier-Brzeska: A Memoir,* New York (New Directions) 1961

Pound, Ezra, *Translations,* New York (New Directions) 1963

Pound, Ezra, *The Cantos,* New York (New Directions) 1970

Pugh, Anthony, *An Introduction to Tensegrity,* Berkeley and Los Angeles (University of California Press) 1976

Reichard, Gladys, *Navaho Religion - A Study of Symbolism,* Princeton, NJ (Bollingen) 1959, 1963

Richard of St. Victor, *The Twelve Patriarchs & The Mystical Ark,* G. A. Zinn trans., Ramsey, NJ (Paulist Press) 1979

Ricoeur, Paul, *The Symbolism of Evil,* New York (Harper & Row) 1967

Rosenstock-Huessy, Eugen, *Speech and Reality,* Norwich, VT (Argo Books) 1970

Rosenstock-Huessy, Eugen, *I Am an Impure Thinker,* Norwich, VT (Argo Books) 1970

Rosenstock-Huessy, Eugen, *The Multiformity of Man,* Norwich, VT (Argo Books) 1973

Schell, Jonathan, *The Fate of the Earth,* New York (Knopf) 1982

Sheldrake, Rupert, *A New Science of Life,* Los Angeles (Tarcher) 1981

Smuts, Jan Christian, *Holism and Evolution,* New York (Macmillan) 1926

Starhawk, *The Spiral Dance,* New York (Harper & Row) 1980

Steiner, George, *After Babel - Aspects of Language and*

Translation, London (Oxford) 1975

Tate, Eugene D., "The Communication Theorist as Pirate and Argonaut: Eugen Rosenstock-Huessy and Communication Theory," *Canadian Journal of Communication*, Vol. 11, No. 3, Summer 1985, pp. 287-307

Tate, Eugene D., "Developments in Communication Theory," *Canadian Journal of Communication*, Vol. 7, No. 3, 1980/81, pp. 58-60

Theall, Donald F., "Messages in McLuhan's Letters: The Communicator as Correspondent," *Canadian Journal of Communication*, Vol. 13, Nos. 3 & 4, 1987, pp. 86-98

Thomas, Lewis, *Lives of a Cell*, New York (Viking) 1974

Tylor, Edward B., *Researches into the Early History of Mankind and the Development of Civilization*, London, 1865, Chicago, 1964

Vachon, R., Ed., *Alternatives au développement*, Montreal (Centre Interculturel Monchanin) 1988

Whorf, Benjamin Lee, *Language, Thought & Reality*, J. B. Carroll, Ed., Cambridge, MA (The M. I. T. Press) 1956

Williams, William Carlos, *Spring & All* (1923); Frontier Press reprint, 1970

###

About the Author

A Californian who makes his home in Montréal, Scott Eastham is currently teaching interdisciplinary and cross-cultural Communication Studies at Concordia University. He received his Ph.D. in Religious Studies from the University of California, and has taught at Catholic University, Georgetown University, Western Maryland College and Sierra Nevada College. His previous books include *Nucleus - Reconnecting Science & Religion in the Nuclear Age* (Bear & Company, 1987), *Wisdom of the Fool - Stories & Poems* (Wyndham Hall, 1985) and *Paradise & Ezra Pound - The Poet as Shaman* (University Press of America, 1983).